Mastering
Book-Keeping

Mastering
Book-Keeping

*A complete guide to the principles and
practice of business accounting*

6th edition

DR PETER MARSHALL

howtobooks

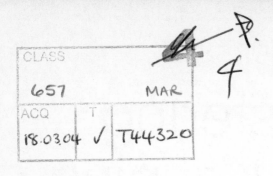
Published by How To Books Ltd, 3 Newtec Place,
Magdalen Road, Oxford OX4 1RE. United Kingdom.
Tel: (01865) 793806. Fax: (01865) 248780.
email: info@howtobooks.co.uk
http://www.howtobooks.co.uk

First edition 1992
Second edition 1995
Third edition 1997
Fourth edition 1999
Fifth edition 2001
Sixth edition 2003

British Library Cataloguing in Publication Data
A catalogue record for this book is available from
the British Library

Produced for How To Books by Deer Park Productions
Typeset by PDQ Typesetting, Newcastle-under-Lyme, Staffs.
Cover design by Baseline Arts Ltd, Oxford
Printed and bound by Cromwell Press, Trowbridge, Wiltshire

NOTE: The material contained in this book is set out in good
faith for general guidance and no liability can be accepted
for loss or expense incurred as a result of relying in particular
circumstances on statements made in the book. The laws and
regulations are complex and liable to change, and readers should
check the current position with the relevant authorities before
making personal arrangements.

Contents

Preface

This book was inspired as much by educational science as by book-keeping. Having had a dual role of business studies writer and educational researcher I have been particularly interested in the way educational science can be applied to this subject, which has, hitherto, been largely missed by the research community.

Other books teach book-keeping in a spatial way assuming that if students understand the page layouts they will naturally understand how to enter them. That is so for people with relatively spatial learning styles, such as accountants tend to have, but it is not the case for those with a more sequential learning style, such as book-keepers so often tend to have. This is a cause of much communication difficulty in classrooms. This book tackles this problem head-on by teaching in a sequential – 'set of rules' – manner.

Although this book aims to teach readers the principles of double entry accounting, it must be acknowledged that there are many small businesses (corner shops, cafés, hairdressers, etc) which do not use this. This edition includes a short section on the kinds of deviations from conventional accounting which a reader may encounter.

This book has been planned to cover the requirements of all the principal book-keeping courses, including the syllabuses of: The London Chamber of Commerce and Industry, The Royal Society of Arts, Pitman, GCSE, the various Open College syllabuses and the relevant parts of the BTech studies courses. It will serve as an invaluable companion to students, trainees and business users alike.

To keep abreast of developments in computer software since the last edition of this book, a section on new developments in electronic book-keeping has been added.

Peter Marshall

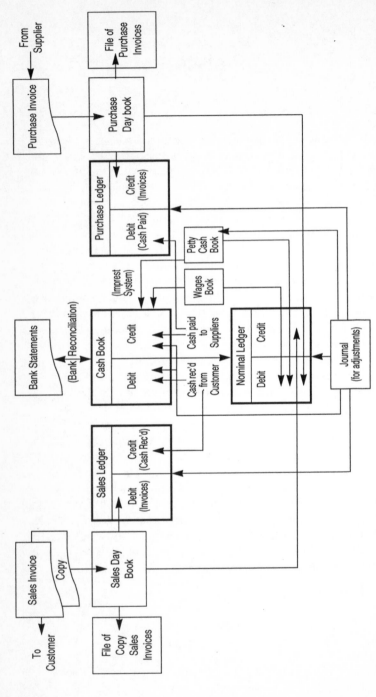

Fig. 1. An overview of business accounts records. Note: The actual records are shown in the boxes. The arrows show the flow of information between the various records. The boxes shown in bold are divisions of the ledger. There is an additional month-end information flow between ledger divisions when cross-referencing is made in folio columns.

8

1 What is double entry book-keeping?

Debit and credit

All transactions have two sides, a **debit** and a **credit**. When a firm sells a TV and sends a bill for payment, for example, on the one hand it has made a sale (which is a credit entry). On the other hand it has gained a liability from the customer (debit entry). That customer is liable to the firm for the money.

The need for two records

Both these transactions need recording separately, because we need:

- a total of sales figures for tax computation and management purposes (to make sure the business is working to plan)

- a cumulative total of money owed by each customer.

A check of accuracy

There is another important advantage of double entry book-keeping. If both sides of each transaction have been recorded then, at any time, if the sums have been done right the debit entries will equal the credit entries. It provides a check of accuracy. An example is as follows:

Example
Suppose A. T. Office Supplies made the following transactions:

> Purchased 6 tables for £60.00 from seller A
> Purchased 10 chairs for £40.00 from seller B
> Sold 1 table for £15.00 to customer A
> Sold 1 chair for £24.00 to customer B
> Received cheque for £15.00 from customer A
> Paid cheque for £60.00 to seller A

The entries would be:

DEBIT	£	CREDIT	£
Purchases	60.00	Seller A	60.00
Purchases	40.00	Seller B	40.00
Customer A	15.00	Sales	39.00
Customer B	24.00		
Bank	15.00	Customer A	15.00
Seller A	60.00	Bank	60.00
	214.00		214.00

JOURNAL

Date 200X	Particulars	Dr.	Cr.
Jan 1	Sundries:		
	Factory Premises	69,500	
	Fixtures and Fittings	1,000	
	Printing Machine	18,000	
	Motor Van	5,000	
	Bank	6,500	
	Capital		100,000

Dr.			Factory premises			*Cr.*
Date 200X	Particulars	Totals	Date 200X	Particulars		Totals
Jan 1	Opening Balance	69,500				

Dr.			Fixtures & Fittings Account			*Cr.*
Date 200X	Particulars	Totals	Date 200X	Particulars		Totals
Jan 1	Opening Balance	1,000				

Dr.			Printing Machine Account			*Cr.*
Date 200X	Particulars	Totals	Date 200X	Particulars		Totals
Jan 1	Opening Balance	18,000				

Dr.			Motor Van Account			*Cr.*
Date 200X	Particulars	Totals	Date 200X	Particulars		Totals
Jan 1	Opening Balance	5,000				

			Capital Account			
Date 200X	Particulars	Totals	Date 200X	Particulars		Totals
			Jan 1	Opening Balance		100,000

CASH BOOK

Receipts					*Payments*				
Date 200X	Particulars	Discount	Cash	Bank	Date	Particulars	Discount	Cash	Bank
Jan 1	Opening Balance			6,500					

Fig. 2. An example of the journalising and posting to the ledger
of the opening figures.

2 Opening the books of account

Assets, liabilities and capital

When opening the books of a new business for the first time we need to list:

- all its assets

- all its liabilities.

By taking away the value of the liabilities from the assets, we can tell how much **capital** the business has at the beginning. In other words:

assets – liabilities = capital

Or to put it another way:

assets = capital + liabilities

Accounts as an equation

The accounts of a business always represent such an equation, in which one side is always exactly balanced by the other side. This balancing list of opening assets, liabilities and capital should then be posted to (i.e. entered in) the relevant ledger accounts, by way of a very useful account book called the **journal**. We will see how to do this when we come to the journal and ledger sections a little later on.

The page on the left shows a typical first page of the journal of a new small printing business, working from a small workshop, and owning a printing machine and delivery van. As you can see, the firm's assets are £100,000, made up of such things as premises, equipment, and £6,500 cash at bank. We keep a separate account for each of these assets—factory premises account, fixtures and fittings account and so on. The cash account we record in the ledger (cash book division); in the example (bottom left) you can see the £6,500 entered in as an 'opening balance'.

Invoice

D. Davidson (Builder)   Delivered to:
1 Main Road   Broad Street
Anytown   Anytown
Lancs   Lancs

P356   20/12/200X

20	Bags of Cement	10.00	200.00
15	5 Litre Tins of White Emulsion	1.00	15.00
80	cwt of Sand	2.00	160.00
40	metres of 4" x 2" Pinewood	1.00	40.00

			415.00
	VAT @ 17½%		72.63
			487.63

E&OE

Fig. 3. Example of an invoice.

Credit Note

D. Davidson (Builder)   Delivered to:
1 Main Road   Broad Street
Anytown   Anytown
Lancs   Lancs

P3756   20/01/200X

60	Door Hinges	0.50	30.00
			30.00
	VAT @ 17½%		5.25
			35.25

E&OE

Fig. 4. Example of a credit note.
E&OE stands for errors and omissions excepted.

3   The day books

Recording daily details: books of prime entry

Double entry accounts are kept in the ledger, but daily details of transactions are not normally entered directly into it; it would become too cluttered and difficult to use. For convenience we first of all enter all the day-to-day details of transactions in other books, called **books of prime entry**. In modern accounting these books are the:

- purchase day book

- purchase returns day book

- sales day book

- sales returns day book

- journal

- cash book

- petty cash book.

Day books or journals

This group of books can also be called either **day books** or **journals**. We will use the term day books here for the four which are identically ruled and most often referred to as day books, that is the purchase day book, purchase returns day book, sales day book and sales returns day book. The word journal we will keep for the journal proper, because of its individual ruling and the others we will call 'books of prime entry'. It is the four day books as defined here, that we will explain in this section.

Source documents for the book-keeper

The sources of information we need to enter into the day books are invoices and credit notes. When a firm receives invoices or credit notes for goods it has purchased they are known as purchase invoices and credit notes inwards respectively. When it sends them out, they are called sales invoices and credit notes outwards. Whether the documents refer to sales or purchases, their format is basically the same. After all, what is a purchase invoice to one party in the transaction is a sales invoice to the other, and similarly for credit notes.

PURCHASE DAY BOOK

Date	Supplier	Inv. No.	Fo.	Net.Inv Value	VAT 17½%	Stationery	Books	Calculators
200X								
Apr 1	Morgan and Baldwyn	4/1	BL6	80.00	14.00	80.00		
3	"			200.00	35.00			200.00
15	S. Jones	4/2	BL5	70.00			70.00	
21	A Singh Wholesale	4/3	BL9	160.00			160.00	
				40.00	7.00	40.00		
30	Morgan and Baldwyn	4/4	BL6	150.00	26.25	150.00		
				700.00	82.25	270.00	230.00	200.00

Fig. 5. How to write up purchases into the purchase day book.

A. Frazer, a retail stationer, makes the following purchases during the month of April 200X:

200X

Apr 1	Morgan and Baldwyn	20 Geometry sets @ £4
3	"	40 Calculators @ £5
15	S. Jones	20 Assorted Books @ £3.50
21	A Singh Wholesale	40 Assorted Books @ £ £4
		80 Bottles of ink @ £0.50
30	Morgan and Baldwyn	25 De-luxe writing cases @ £6

Figure 5 shows how he writes up the transactions in the purchase day book.

4 The purchase day book

The **purchase day book** is one of the day books mentioned. It is where we first enter up all our purchases on credit. The book itself is not part of 'the accounts': it is just one of the sources from which the accounts will be written up later on.

How to write up the purchase day book
What you need:

- the purchase day book
- the invoices for the period (day, week etc).

First, sort the invoices into date order. Next, write or stamp a purchase invoice number on each one. (This is not the invoice number printed on the document when the firm receives it; that is the sales invoice number of the firm which sent it.) The idea is to help the book-keeper find an invoice easily if he has to look up details of an old transaction.

Many firms keep a list of consecutive numbers for this purpose. Others use a two-part number made up of the month number and a number from a consecutive list for that month.

Step-by-step
1. Write the year of entry once, at the head of entries to be made for that year. There is no need then to keep writing the year against each individual entry. This helps to keep the page neat and uncluttered. Do the same for the month, and then the day, as in the example on the opposite page:

    Apr   1
              3
            15
            21
            30

2. Enter the supplier's name, e.g. Morgan and Baldwyn.
3. Enter your own purchase invoice number e.g. 4/1.
4. Enter net invoice total, e.g. £80.00. (Net means after deduction of any trade discounts and not including VAT; we will come to these later.)
5. Enter the VAT, e.g. £14.00.
6. If analysis columns are in use, also enter the net amount of each invoice under the correct heading, e.g. 'stationery'.
7. When required (e.g. monthly) total each column. You will then be able to post (transfer) the totals to the ledger.

S. JONES (WHOLESALE STATIONERY SUPPLIES) LTD
210 Barton High Street, Barton, Barshire

Credit Note No: SJ /02206   10/2/200X

To authorised return of faulty
desk diaries   200.00

VAT @ 17½%   35.00
                                                              235.00

Name of customer
D. Davidson
1 Main Street
Anytown
Lancs.

Fig. 6. Example of a credit note inwards.

PURCHASE RETURNS DAYBOOK

Date	Supplier	C/N No	Net Inv. Value	VAT 17½%	Stationery	Books	Cards	Machines
200X								
Feb10	S.Jones	2/1	200.00	35.00	200.00			
14	Morgan & Baldwyn	2/2	270.00			270.00		
25	A. Singh	2/3	230.00	40.25			15.00	215.00
			700.00	75.25	200.00	270.00	15.00	215.00

Fig. 7. Example of the same credit entered into the
purchase returns daybook.

5   The purchase returns day book

Returning unwanted goods

When a firm buys goods or services on credit, it records the details in the purchase day book, as we saw on the previous pages. Sometimes, however, it has to return what it has bought to the supplier. For example the goods may be faulty, or arrived damaged. In this case, the firm obtains a **credit note** from the supplier, and the value of the credit note is then entered up in the purchase returns day book.

All the points which apply to the purchase day book also apply to the purchase returns day book. Even the ruling is identical, though of course the transaction details may be different. So once you have become familiar with the ruling of a typical purchase day book, you will also have a picture of the purchase returns day book in your mind.

Example

Look at the example on the opposite page. We purchased a quantity of desk diaries from S. Jones (Wholesale Stationery Supplies Ltd), and unfortunately found that some of them were faulty. We told them about the problem and they agreed that we could return them. S. Jones then issued us with a credit note for the value of the faulty goods, plus VAT, a total of £235.00. The credit note is dated 10th February. We now enter the details of this credit note in our purchase returns day book as shown opposite.

1.   On the far left we enter the date, followed by the name of the supplier.

2.   In the third column we enter our own credit note number from our own sequences of numbers, in this case 2/1 meaning February, credit note number one. (We do not enter S. Jones' own number SJ/02206).

3.   In the correct columns we then enter the net amount of the credit, i.e. excluding VAT — £200.00 — and the VAT element of £35.00 in the VAT column.

4.   If our purchase returns day book has additional analysis columns, we 'analyse' the net amount into the correct column, in this case stationery.

The additional analysis columns can be useful, because they help us to check the value of each category of goods returned.

Entwhistle & Co – Builders Merchants
Ferry Yard, Anytown, Anyshire

To: D. Davidson (Builder)   2nd January 200X
    1 Main Street
    Anytown
    Lancs

INVOICE No:-   **501**

100 English facing bricks @ 28p	£ 28.00
24 breeze blocks @ 50p	12.00
Assorted cut timber	320.00
Screws, nails and ironmongery	40.00
5 rolls vinyl wallpaper @ £ 3	15.00
	415.00
VAT @ 17½%	72.63
Total	487.63

Terms strictly 30 days net

Fig. 8. Example of a sales invoice.

SALES DAY BOOK

Date	Customer	Inv. No.	Net.Inv. Value	VAT 17½%	Bricklyr Supplies	Carptry Supplies	Decor Supplies	Roofing Supplies
200X								
Jan 2	D. Davidson	SO1	415.00	72.63	40.00	360.00	15.00	
4	Kahn & Kahn	SO2	30.00	5.25		30.00		
5	JBC Roofing	SO3	250.00	43.75				250.00
			695.00	121.63	40.00	390.00	15.00	250.00

Fig. 9. The same sales invoice duly entered into the sales day book.

6 The sales day book

A. Frazer records his sales

Let us suppose that A. Frazer is a business stationery supplier. He makes the following sales on monthly credit account during the month of June 200X:

200X
Jun 1 Edwards' Garage 1 gross of white foolscap envelopes = £4.00
                       1 gross of small manilla envelopes = £4.00
      6 A. K. Insurance
            Services   1 gross of large envelopes = £10.00
      8 J.B.C. Roofing 4 Calculators @ £12.50 ea
     30 F. Evans   20 Foolscap note pads = £21.60

Let's suppose that, like many firms, A. Frazer has his sales invoices pre-printed with numbers in a chronological sequence and that the above sales were billed on invoice numbers 961/2/3 and 4. He would write the invoice dates followed by the names of the customers in the first two columns of his sales day book. In the next column he would enter the net invoice values (i.e. excluding VAT), and in the next the amounts of VAT charged on each invoice. Further to the right, he would then 'analyse' the net amounts into handy reference columns. (This analysis will be useful to him later, as he will be able to tell quickly what value of his sales were for stationery, what for calculators, and what for any other categories which he may decide to have analysis columns for.)

Date	Supplier	Inv. No	Net Inv. Value	VAT 17½%	Statnry	Calcs.
200X						
Jun 1	Edwards' Garage	961	8.00	1.40	8.00	
6	A.K. Insurance Servs	2	10.00	1.75	10.00	
8	J.B.C. Roofing	3	50.00	8.75		50.00
30	F. Evans	4	21.60	3.78	21.60	
			89.60	15.68	39.60	50.00

Fig. 10. Extract from A. Frazer's sales day book.

```
CREDIT NOTE No: 0135                    8 March 200X


To authorised return of                      £    p
5 x 10 Litre cans of white gloss paint       50.00
returned as faulty
VAT @ 17½%                                     8.75
                                              58.75



┌                         ┐
  Name of customer
  D. Davidson (Builder)
  1, Main Street
  Anytown
  Lancs
└                         ┘
```

Fig. 11. Example of a credit note inwards.

SALES RETURNS DAY BOOK

Date	Customer	C/N No	Net Inv Value	VAT 17½%	Bricklyr Supplies	Carptry Supplies	Decor Supplies
200X							
Mar 8	D. Davidson	135	50.00	8.75			50.00
10	J.B.C. Roofing	6	60.00	10.50	60.00		
			110.00	19.25	60.00		50.00

Fig. 12. The same credit note outwards duly entered
into the sales returns day book.

7   The sales returns day book

When a customer asks for a credit

When a firm sells goods or services on credit, it records the details in the sales day book, as we saw on the previous pages. Sometimes, however, the customer has to return what he has bought. For example the goods may be faulty, or arrived damaged. In this case, the firm sends a **credit note** to the customer, and the value of the credit note is then entered up in the sales returns day book.

All the points which apply to the sales day book also apply to the sales returns day book, even the ruling is identical, though of course the transaction details may be different. So once you have become familiar with the ruling of a typical sales day book, you will also have a picture of the sales returns day book in your mind.

Example

Look at the example on the opposite page. We sold 50 litres of white gloss paint to D. Davidson (Builders) who unfortunately found them to be faulty. They returned the goods to us and we issued them with a credit note for the value plus VAT, a total of £58.75. The credit note is dated 8 March 200X. We now enter the details of this credit note in our sales returns day book as shown opposite.

1. On the far left we enter the date, followed by the name of the customer.

2. In the third column we enter the credit note number (this is usually pre-printed on credit notes outwards, but if not it must be allocated from a chronological sequence).

3. In the correct columns we then enter the amounts of the credit, i.e. excluding VAT— £50.00—and the VAT element of £8.75 in the VAT column.

4. If our sales returns day book has additional analysis columns, we 'analyse' the net amount into the correct one, in this case *Decorators' supplies*.

The additional analysis columns can be useful, because they help us to check the value of each category of goods returned.

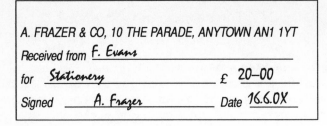

A. FRAZER & CO, 10 THE PARADE, ANYTOWN AN1 1YT

Received from *F. Evans*

for *Stationery* £ *20—00*

Signed *A. Frazer* Date *16.6.0X*

BARSHIRE BANK PLC
Barshire House, Barton *1.6.* 20 *0X*

Pay *D. DAVIDSON*

Twenty one pounds only

21.00

A.K. INSURANCE

B. Jones

CASH BOOK

Dr. (Receipts)								*(Payments) Cr.*	
Date	Particulars	Fo.	Discount	Cash	Bank	Date	Particulars	Fo.	Discount	Cash	Bank

Date	Particulars	Fo.	Discount	Cash	Bank	Date	Particulars	Fo.	Discount	Cash	Bank
June 1	Balance	b/d		50.00	1,750.00	Jun 1	Razi & Thaung	BL3			40.00
2	Edwards Garage	SL2	2.50		97.50	1	D. Davidson	BL5			21.00
8	Cash Sales	NL2		7.50		9	A.T. Office Supplies	BL4		100.00	
9	C.Jones	SL5			12.50	12	Cash	¢			290.00
12	Bank	¢		290.00		14	Wages	NL8		240.00	
15	J.B.C. Roofing	SL7		110.00		14	Petty Cash	PCB3		50.00	
16	Cash Sales	NL2		20.00		20	M. Bandura	BL6		30.00	
24	Eliot Transport	SL8	5.00		200.00	22	L. Cleaves	BL12	4.87		190.00
24	Morgan & Baldwyn	SL1			42.50	22	Van den Burgh	BL7			200.00
30	Cash	¢			7.50	30	Interest and				
							bank charges				20.00
						30	Bank	¢		7.50	
						30	Balance	c/d		50.00	1,349.00
			7.50	477.50	2,110.00				4.87	477.50	2,110.00

Fig. 13. Examples of cash book entries concerning money received, and a payment by cheque.

8 The cash book

What is the cash book?

The cash book is where we record the firm's cash and cheque transactions. In it we record all the payments coming in and all the payments going out. Like the four day books it is a book of prime entry: it is the first place we record a transaction. However, unlike the day books, it is also a book of account, i.e. part of the ledger. The cash book and petty cash book are the only ones with this dual status.

Recording cash and bank transactions

The cash book is where we first record the details of cash and banking transactions. This includes all cash or cheques received from such customers as Mr Jones or JBC Roofing (see opposite) or indeed from anyone else, and all cash or cheques paid out to suppliers or to anyone else (disbursements). Banks debit firms directly for their services—they don't send out invoices for payment of interest and bank charges. The firm must record details of these amounts in the cash book as soon as it knows them, for example from the bank statement which shows them.

Source documents

To write up the cash book we need:

- Cheque book stubs (counterfoils) and paying-in book stubs (counterfoils) for all transactions which involve the bank account.
- Any bank advice slips, bank statements or other information received from the bank from time to time. This might for example include a letter advising that a customer's cheque has been returned unpaid by his bank owing to lack of funds, or information on standing orders, direct debits or bank charges and so on: anything that tells us about any payments going out from, or receipts coming into, the firm's account.
- Cash purchase invoices, receipts for cash paid out, and copies of receipts given for cash paid in.
- Any payment advice slips which arrived with cheques or cash received: these will show for example whether an early settlement discount has been claimed.

Entering debits and credits

All the cash and cheques we receive are entered on the left hand side of the cash book (debits). All the cheques we write and cash we pay is entered on the right hand side (credits).

CASH BOOK

Dr.									Cr.
Date	Particulars	Fo.	Cash	Bank	Date	Particulars	Fo.	Cash	Bank
200X					200X				
Mar 1	Balance	b/d		1,500.00	Mar 28	S. Jones	BL6		48.60
19	Cash Sales	NL4	81.00		31	Salaries	NL9		600.00
31	Bank	¢	303.16		31	Cash	¢		303.16
					31	Wages	NL14	384.16	
					31	Balance	c/d	0.00	548.24
			384.16	1,500.00				384.16	1,500.00
Apl 1	Balance	b/d	0.00	548.24					

Fig. 14. Entering details of cash and bank transactions
into the cash book.

Suppose the cash and banking transactions of A. Frazer for the month of March 200X were as follows:

1 Opening balance Cash: £0, Bank: £1,500.00 (in favour)

		£
March19	Received from cash sales	81.00
28	Paid S. Jones A/C by cheque	48.60
31	Secretary's salary cheque	600.00
31	Drew cash	303.16
31	Paid wages in cash	384.16

The cash book entries should look as they are in Figure 14.

9 The cash book: money paid in

Cash book entry step-by-step

1. Turn to your first receipt counterfoil for the period you are handling (day, week, month). Record, in the first column of the cash book on the far left the date of the transaction. To help keep the page neat and uncluttered, just enter the year once at the top of all the entries for that year. Do the same for the start of each new month.
2. Write the payer's name in the second column (Cash Sales in the example opposite).
3. The third column is for the folio reference which you will enter later. Leave it blank at this stage.
4. In the fourth column (not used in example) enter the amount of any early settlement discount.
5. In the fifth column (cash) enter the amount of cash received, £81.00.
6. Now turn to your paying-in book counterfoils and do exactly the same—except for one small difference: enter the amounts in the sixth (bank) column this time. Enter in the first (date) column the date of the bank lodgement as shown on the front of the counterfoil. The date written in ink by the payer-in (the cashier) might be different from the bank branch stamp on the counterfoil; the paying-in book might have been written up the day before the lodgment, and lodged in a nightsafe at the bank after the close of business, to be paid in properly the next day. Where there is a difference, you should use the date shown on the bank's stamp.
7. Turn the counterfoil for the period over and look on its reverse side. Each counterfoil represents a payment into the bank of a sum of money in cash and/or cheques; it should bear the names of people from whom the cheques have been received (the drawers). Enter in the second column of the cash book (name column) the first name from this list.
8. Again, the third column is for the folio reference, which you will enter later. Leave it blank for now.
9. Enter in the fourth column (discounts) the details of any discount allowed.
10. Enter in the sixth column the actual amount of the cheque.
11. Repeat steps 6 to 10 for all the cheques in the list.
12. Now enter the cash paid in to the bank, if any.
13. Write the word 'cash' in the second column (since it is the cashier who is paying it in).
14. Enter amount in the sixth column (bank column).

CASH BOOK OF A. FRAZER

Dr.								Cr.		
Date Particulars 200X	Fo.	Discount	Cash	Bank	Date Particulars 200X		Fo.	Discount	Cash	Bank
Aug 1 Balance	b/d		50.00		Aug 1	Balance	b/d			1,100.00
2 Edwards Garage	SL60	0.72		27.88	30	Wages	NL8			800.00
12 Razi & Thaung	SL9	10.07		392.43	30	A.T. Office				
20 Morgan & Baldwyn	SL11			560.63		Suppls	BL5	5.01		195.50
					30	F. Evans	BL6			258.00
31 Balance	c/d			1,372.56	31	Balance	c/d		50.00	
		10.79	50.00	2,353.50				5.01	50.00	2,353.50
Sept 1 Balance	b/d		50.00		Sep 1	Balance	b/d			1,372.56

Fig. 15. A. Frazer's cash book.

Notes

The balance of A. Frazer's cash as at 1st August 200X was £50.00 and there was a bank overdraft of £1,100. On 2nd August a cheque was received from Edwards' Garage for £27.88 in full settlement of its bill of £28.60. On checking, it is found that discount has been properly deducted. On the 12th a cheque was received from Razi and Thaung for £392.43 in full settlement of their a/c in the sum of £402.50, after properly deducting 2½% discount for settlement within 7 days. On the 20th a cheque was received from Morgan and Baldwyn in the sum of £560.63 in full settlement of a/c in the sum of £575.00, after deducting 2½% discount for payment within 7 days. On checking it is found that the cheque is dated 14 days after the invoice date. On the 30th £800.00 cash was drawn for wages, a cheque for £195.50 was paid to A. T. Office Supplies after deducting 2½% for payment within 28 days and a cheque for £258 was paid to F. Evans.

Write up his cash book for the month. (Worked answer below.)

1. No discount has been entered for Morgan and Baldwyn as they were not eligible for the discount they claimed. Only £560.63 would, therefore, be deducted from their ledger account and they would remain indebted to the firm for the remaining £14.37.

2. If the cheque for £195.50 takes into account a 2½% discount then the discount figure will be £5.12, since if £195.50 = 97.5% then 1% =

$$\frac{£195.50}{97.5}$$

= £2.00½ and 100% = £2.00½ × 100 = £200.50, of which 2½% = £5.01

3. It has been regarded as unnecessary to debit the £800 drawn from the bank to cash since it went straight out again in wages; the debit entry has, thus, been made directly to Wages Account.

10   The cash book: money paid out

Posting to the credit page

Now we need to do our first piece of double entry book-keeping. Since the bank has been debited with the money the cashier paid in, the cashier must be credited with the same amount. Otherwise, the cashier will appear to remain indebted for a sum he no longer has.

Step-by-step

1. Enter the date of the paying-in slip in the date column of the right hand (credit page) of the cash book.
2. In the second (name) column, enter the word 'Bank', since it is the Bank which is taking the money from the cashier.
3. In the fifth (cash) column, enter the amount of the payment. You have now given the cashier credit for that amount—and so you should! He no longer has it: he has given it to the Bank.
4. Now let's do the other credit side entries. Take the first of the receipt vouchers for cash paid out for the period (day, week, month). Enter the date (taken from the receipt voucher) in the appropriate column of the right hand page (see step 1 on the previous page).
5. In the second column enter the name of the person to whom the cash was paid.
6. Discount details probably won't be relevant here; such discounts arise from early settlement of credit accounts, usually by cheque rather than by cash. If any such account was settled in cash, the cashier would know about it: he would have been the one to arrange payment. In such cases enter the details in the fourth (discount) column.
7. In the fifth column enter the amount of cash paid out.
8. Turn to the first cheque book counterfoil for the period. In the first column of the right hand (credit) page, enter the cheque date.
9. In the second column enter the name of the payee (the person to whom the cheque is payable).
10. In the fourth column enter details of any discount received. You will find this from the copy of the payment advice slip outwards.
11. In the sixth (bank) column, enter the amount of the cheque.
12. When required, total both the debit and credit columns for both cash and bank. Enter balancing items, so that both sides add up to the same figure, narrating them 'balance c/d'.
13. Bring down the balancing items on the opposite sides as the opening balances for the next period, narrating them 'balance b/d'.

BANK RECONCILIATION
as at 30 June 200X

Balance as per Bank Statement (in favour)			880.00
Deduct cheques drawn but not as yet presented for payment:			
	Smith	30.00	
	Jones	40.00	
	Clarke	50.00	120.00
			760.00
Add Lodgement 30 June not yet showing on Bank Statement			250.00
Corrected balance as per Bank Statement			1,010.00
Balance as per Cashbook (in favour)			910.00
Add Customer account paid directly into the bank:			
	Watson		180.00
			1,090.00
Deduct dishonoured cheque:			
	Davies		50.00
			1,040.00
Deduct standing order paid but not yet recorded in Cash Book:			
	Wilson & Smith		30.00
Corrected balance as per Cash Book			1,010.00

Fig. 16. Example of a bank reconciliation.

11 Disagreeing with the bank

Cash book versus bank statement

Every cashier tries to keep the cash book as accurate and up-to-date as possible. Many receipts and many payments may have to be entered up each day. Then, at regular intervals, the firm receives bank statements from the bank—weekly, monthly or quarterly. Unfortunately, the balance shown on the cash book hardly ever agrees with the one shown on the bank statement! There can be various reasons for this.

Noting unpresented cheques

When you get the bank statement and compare the balance with that shown in your cash book, you'll see that some cheques you drew have not yet been presented to the bank for payment: they simply don't appear on the bank statement at all, as yet. The cashier enters cheque transactions within a day or two of handling the cheques; but it could be days or even weeks before the payee presents them to your bank for payment.

Noting bank lodgements

Payments into the bank will have been recorded in the cash book, but if they haven't yet been recorded by the bank they won't appear on the bank statement. This could happen, for example, if a bank statement was sent out between the time the cashier lodged the bankings in the night safe and the time he actually paid them in over the counter.

Automatic payments

Payments by direct debit or standing order may have been omitted by the cashier, but they will still appear on the bank statement.

Bank charges and interest

A cashier may know nothing about these until the bank statement arrives, containing the details.

Returned cheques

A customer's cheque may have been returned unpaid—'bounced' in popular jargon. The cash book will show the money having been received, but the bank won't have received funds for the cheque; so the statement will show a contra entry.

Errors

The cashier could simply have made an error. Bank errors can happen, but they are rare.

BANK RECONCILIATION AS AT *(date...)*

	£ p	
Balance as per bank statement	500.00	(in favour)
Deduct cheque drawn but not yet		
presented for payment: S. Jones	200.00	
Amended balance as per bank statement	300.00	(in favour)
Balance as per cash book	320.00	(in favour)
Add customer's account		
paid by telephone banking (M. Bandura)	40.00	
	360.00	(in favour)
Deduct dishonoured cheque (D. Davidson)	10.00	
	350.00	(in favour)
Deduct bank charges	50.00	
Amended balance as per cash book	300.00	(in favour)

Fig. 17. Worked example of a bank reconciliation statement.

On comparing A. Frazer's bank balance as per bank statement with his bank balance as per cash book, it is found that the former shows £500 in favour while the latter shows £320 in favour. In looking for the reasons we find that a cheque drawn by D. Davidson in favour of the firm in the sum of £10.00 has been dishonoured, a cheque drawn by the firm in favour of S. Jones for £200 has not yet been presented by his bank for payment, bank charges have been made in the sum of £50 and a customer's (M. Bandura's) bill of £40.00 has been paid via telephone banking and the cashier was not aware of this. Figure 17 shows how we would write up a Bank Reconciliation Statement.

12   The bank reconciliation

If a discrepancy arose from just one source it would be easy enough to deal with, but usually there are several discrepancies, some distorting the credit side and some distorting the debit side, and liable to cause confusion.

To remove this confusion, and explain the discrepancies, the cashier draws up a bank reconciliation statement. The cashier, after all, is responsible for the firm's money, so if the bank statement disagrees with his cash book balance, he must clearly show the reason why.

There are three ways of reconciling the two accounts:

1. Reconcile cash book to bank statement: starting with the closing cash book balance, and check through step-by-step towards the bank balance, explaining the discrepancies as we go.

2. Reconcile the bank statement to the cash book: the opposite process.

3. Correct all the errors and omissions on both the cashier's part and the bank's part, showing how we did it, until we end up with the same balance from both viewpoints.

The third way is usually the best since it is easier to understand. We'll see how to write up a bank reconciliation statement, step-by-step, on the following pages.

BANK RECONCILIATION AS AT (*date...*)

	£ p
Balance as per bank statement	600.00 (overdrawn)
Add cheque drawn but not yet	
presented for payment: S. Jones	200.00
Amended balance as per bank statement	800.00 (overdrawn)
Balance as per cash book	780.00 (overdrawn)
Add dishonoured cheque: D. Davidson	10.00
	790.00 (overdrawn)
Add bank charges	50.00
	840.00 (overdrawn)
Deduct customer's account	
paid by telephone banking: M. Bandura	40.00
Amended balance as per cash book	800.00 (overdrawn)

Fig. 18. Another worked example of a bank reconciliation statement.

Suppose the same circumstances as in the worked example were true except that the balance as per bank statement was £600 overdrawn and the balance as per Cash Book was £780 overdrawn. Figure 18 shows what the bank reconciliation would look like.

13   How to prepare a bank reconcilation statement

What you need:

- the cash book

- the bank statements for the period (week, month, quarter).

Remember, a page of figures can be bewildering to your reader, who may not understand book-keeping as well as you, or have the time or patience to make sense of muddled words and figures. Simplicity and clarity should be your goal. Head all your cash columns £ and p to avoid having to write these symbols against every single entry. Likewise, when writing dates record the month once only, followed by the individual days. Put a clear heading against the left of each line of your figures. You will probably need two cash columns, one for sub-totalling particular types of transactions. For example, if there are three unpresented cheques you would add their values in a left hand column, and place the subtotal in a main right hand column.

Bank reconciliation step-by-step

1. Compare the balances of the bank statement and the cash book as at the end of the accounting period you are checking. If they disagree then a bank reconciliation will be needed. Proceed as follows.

2. Check off each payment listed in the cash book against the bank statement. Tick each one in pencil in the cash book, and on the bank statement, as you go. As you will see, items on the credit side of your cash book appear on the debit side of the bank statement, and vice versa. This is because the same account is seen from two opposite viewpoints: the cash book from the firm's, the bank statement from the bank's.

3. Can you see on the statement any standing orders (STOs), direct debits (DDRs) or bank charges? These items may not have been recorded in your cash book as yet. Also, are there any returned ('bounced') cheques? If there are, they will appear as consecutive entries, identical but appearing on opposite sides (*Dr* and *Cr*) and will be annotated 'contra entry'.

```
                    BANK RECONCILIATION
                     as at 30 June 200X

Balance as per Bank Statement (in favour)              880.00
Deduct cheques drawn but not as yet
presented for payment:
                        Smith     30.00
                        Jones     40.00
                        Clarke    50.00
                                                       120.00
                                                       760.00
Add Lodgement 30 June not yet showing
on Bank Statement:                                     250.00
                                                     1,010.00
Deduct customer account paid
directly into the bank:
                        Watson                         180.00
                                                       830.00
Add dishonoured cheque:
                        Davies                          50.00
                                                       880.00
Add Standing Order paid but not yet
recorded in Cash Book:
                        Wilson & Smith                  30.00
Balance as per Cash Book                               910.00
```

```
                    BANK RECONCILIATION
                     as at 30 June 200X

Balance as per Cash Book (in favour)                   910.00
Add cheques drawn but not as yet
presented for payment:
                        Smith     30.00
                        Jones     40.00
                        Clarke    50.00
                                                       120.00
                                                     1,030.00
Deduct dishonoured cheque:
                        Davies                          50.00
                                                       980.00
Deduct Lodgement 30 June not yet showing
on Bank Statement:                                     250.00
                                                       730.00
Deduct Standing Order paid but not yet
recorded in Cash Book:
                        Wilson and Smith                30.00
                                                       700.00
Add customer account paid
directly into the bank:
                        Watson                         180.00
Balance as per Bank Statement (in favour)              880.00
```

Fig 19. The bank reconciliation method advised has been chosen for its simplicity and clarity. Above are worked examples of the two alternatives referred to on page 33; use them only if specifically requested by an examiner or employer.

13 How to prepare a bank reconciliation—cont.

4. Take a sheet of A4 paper and begin by writing: 'Balance as per bank statement.' State whether it is 'in favour' or 'overdrawn' (see example opposite). It is important to use a term such as 'in favour' rather than 'in credit', since 'in credit' is ambiguous here: an 'in credit' bank balance means you are 'in the black'; but an 'in credit' balance in the cash book means you are 'in the red'. The terms in favour and overdrawn overcome this ambiguity, since they mean the same from both viewpoints, the firm's and the bank's.

5. Record the 'Balance as per bank statement', with the amount. Then list all the errors and omissions on the bank's part, in groups, for example listing unpresented cheques first, and then any unshown lodgements. Write your additions and deductions as you go to show what difference they would have made to the bank statement if such errors or omissions had not occurred.

6. When you have listed all the errors and omissions, write against your final figure: 'Corrected bank statement balance'.

7. Now do the same for the cashier. Begin by writing: 'Balance as per Cash Book.' Then list all the errors and omissions on the cashier's part. They won't of course be the same ones. For example the bank won't have recorded unpresented cheques, but the cashier will. When your two corrected totals are the same, the job of reconciliation is done. There is more about Bank Reconciliations on page 158.

You have now crossed from single entry book-keeping into double entry accounting, since the cash book bridges a gap between these two, being both a book of prime entry, and part of the double entry system.

In most accounts offices the keeping of the cash book is a specialised job. It is the task of the cashier, a position of considerable responsibility and attracting a higher salary than that of a day book clerk. For those of you already working in accounts offices, mastering this section could soon gain you promotion and pay rises.

PETTY CASH BOOK

Dr   *Cr*

Receipts	Fo.	Date	Details	Rec	Total	Motor Exp.	Travlg Exp.	Postage	Statnry	Cleaning
		200X								
50.00	CB5	May 1	Cash							
		1	Petrol	5/1	10.00	10.00				
		2	Fares	5/2	3.20		3.20			
		5	Petrol	5/3	8.00	8.00				
		8	Postage	5/4	9.00			9.00		
		17	Stationery	5/5	1.30				1.30	
		22	Fares	5/6	1.40		1.40			
		25	Fares	5/7	1.40		1.40			
		26	Petrol	5/8	7.00	7.00				
		31	Cleaning	5/9	4.00					4.00
		31	Fares	5/10	1.40		1.40			
		31	Postage	5/11	1.80			1.80		
					48.50	25.00	7.40	10.80	1.30	4.00
						NL8	NL9	NL15	NL17	NL18
48.50	CB6	31	Cash							
		31	Balance c/d		50.00					
98.50					98.50					
50.00		Jun 1	Balance b/d							

Fig. 20. Example of a completed petty cash book page.

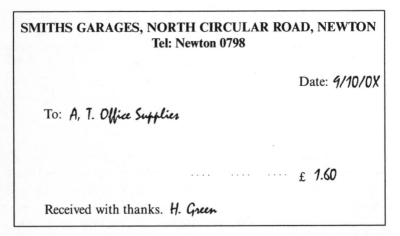

Fig. 21. Example of a simple cash purchase invoice, showing the supplier, goods or services supplied, date, and payment.

14 The petty cash book

The petty cash float
The petty cashier looks after a small float such as £50 or £100 in notes and coins. It is used to pay for miscellaneous small office expenses such as staff travel and hotel accommodation, window cleaning, or small office items needed quickly. The petty cashier keeps account of all such transactions in the petty cash book.

Using the imprest system
From time to time the cashier will reimburse the petty cashier for the amount he has spent on his firm's behalf: his float is replenished to the original amount. This is called an **imprest system**, and the original amount of the float e.g. £50 is called the **imprest amount**.

Without a petty cash book, cash expenditure on lots of very small items would mean making entries in the ledger, for each item of expense. But by using the petty cash book, such items can be analysed into useful columns which can be totalled up monthly, and just these totals—not all the details—posted to the ledger.

A helpful analysis
Even if the firm is small, and the cashier keeps the petty cash book himself, it is still a very useful means of analysing and totalling office expenditure. Otherwise all such expenditure would have to be entered in the cash book and later posted individually to the ledger. The cash book, remember, has no analysis facility for double entry book-keeping. The analysis columns of the petty cash book act as a book of prime entry for the expenses in which the petty cashier becomes involved. From here they are later posted to the expense accounts in the ledger.

Dual status of the petty cash book
The petty cash book, like the cash book, usually has a dual status: it is both a book of prime entry and part of the ledger. However, some firms treat it purely as a book of prime entry, to record transactions involving notes and coins. They then write up a 'petty cash account' in their general ledger. Here, however, we will treat it as part of the ledger. Unless told otherwise, you should do the same.

Like the other books of prime entry, such as the day books, the petty cash book usually has a few helpful analysis columns. But since it is also part of the ledger, it also needs to have both debit and credit columns.

Dr.			PETTY CASH BOOK						Cr.
Receipts	Fo.	Date	Details	Rec. No.	Total	Stnry	Trav. Exp.	Tel.	Cleang.
		200X							
50.00	CB1	Jan 1	Bank						
		6	Stationery	1/01	1.50	1.50			
		17	Trvlg Exp.	1/02	2.00		2.00		
		26	Telephone	1/03	0.50			0.50	
		28	Wndw Clnr	1/04	8.00				8.00
					12.00	1.50	2.00	0.50	8.00
12.00	CB1	31				NL4	NL6	NL8	NL9
		31	Balance c/d		50.00				
62.00					62.00				
50.00		Feb 1	Balance b/d						

Fig. 22.

1. Suppose A. Frazer has only just started up in business and intends to use an imprest system for his petty cash transactions. (The firm's estimated turnover is below the VAT threshold so it does not intend to register as taxable. There is, therefore, no need to account for VAT in the petty cash book.) The transactions during its first month are as follows. Write up his petty cash book for the month.

Jan	1	Received cheque from cashier £50
	6	Paid for staples and glue £1.50
	17	Paid travelling expenses £2.00
	26	Refunded phone-call expenses 50p
	28	Paid window cleaner £8.00
	31	Received cheque from cashier to replenish the fund to the imprest amount of £50.00

2. A. Frazer is a Taxable firm for VAT purposes; this means that the VAT aspects of its transactions have to be recorded in its books. Suppose the firm's Petty Cash transactions for the month of December 200X are as follows. Write up his petty cash book for the month, using the imprest system. Assume, for the purpose of this exercise, that there is currently only one VAT rate in operation and that is 10%.

Opening balance £100.00, Dec 10 paid travelling expenses £20.00, Dec 15 refunded petrol expenses £10.00 and paid cleaner £16.00, Dec 21 bought parcel tape £1.85, Dec 31 received cheque from cashier to replenish the fund to the imprest figure of £100.00

Dr.			PETTY CASH BOOK							Cr.
Receipts	Fo.	Date	Details	Rec. No.	Total	VAT	Trvlg. Exp.	Motor Exp.	Wages	Stnry.
		200X								
100.00		Dec 1	Balance b/d							
		10	Trv. Exp	12/01	20.00		20.00			
		15	Petrol	12/02	10.00	0.90		9.10		
			Cleaner	12/03	16.00				16.00	
		21	Prcl Tape	12/04	1.85	0.16				1.69
					47.85	1.06	20.00	9.10	16.00	1.69
47.85	CB15	31	Balance c/d		100.00	NL11	NL6	NL7	NL5	NL9
147.85					147.85					
		200X								
100.00		Jan 1	Balance c/d							

Fig. 23.

15 How to write up the petty cash book

What you need:

- the petty cash book

- all the cash purchase invoices for the period.

Preparation: numbering and dating

Sort all your cash purchase invoices (receipts) into date order, and number them. (The numbers already printed on them won't do: they are cash sales invoice numbers of the firms that issued them and no uniformity between them can be expected.) You need to give them consecutive numbers from your own numbering system, so that you can file them chronologically for each period. Many firms keep a list of such numbers for this purpose. Others give them a two part number made up of the month number (e.g. 3 for March) and a number from a consecutive list for that month.

Value Added Tax (VAT)

The VAT may not be shown as a separate item on cash purchase invoices for small amounts. If not, the petty cashier will need to calculate the VAT content, if any, of each invoice total (see page 153). HM Customs & Excise publish details of current VAT applications and rates, but a little experience will save the petty cashier having to check this every time. Briefly, if the current VAT rate is $17\frac{1}{2}\%$, the VAT content of such an invoice is worked out like this:

Invoice amount:	£100
Equivalent to:	100% net amount plus $17\frac{1}{2}\%$ VAT
Therefore VAT element:	$\dfrac{17\frac{1}{2}\%}{100\% + 17\frac{1}{2}\%}$ or $\dfrac{17.5 \times 100}{117.5}$
Answer	£14.89 (not £17.50!)

Opening a new petty cashbook

When starting a new petty cash system (i.e. opening a new petty cash book) a sum of money will be entrusted as a float to the petty cashier, let's say £50.00. He immediately enters this on the debit (left) side, because he now 'owes' the cashier that amount.

PETTY CASH BOOK

Receipts	Fo.	Date	No.	Details	Rec	Total	VAT	Trav. Exp.	Stnry	Motor Exp.	Post
		200X									
100.00	CB6	Feb 1		Cash							
			1	Fares	2/1	5.00		5.00			
			2	Envelopes	2/2	7.00	1.04		5.96		
			4	Petrol	2/3	8.00	1.19			6.81	
			7	Petrol	2/4	9.00	1.34			7.66	
			16	Postage	2/5	6.00	0.89				5.11
			18	Fares	2/6	3.00		3.00			
			19	Fares	2/7	3.00		3.00			
			25	Petrol	2/8	7.00	1.04			5.96	
			26	Postage	2/9	4.50					4.50
			27	Staples	2/10	2.00	0.30		1.70		
			28	String	2/11	3.50	0.52		2.98		
58.00						58.00	6.32	11.00	10.64	20.43	9.61
158.00							NL8	NL6	NL14	NL11	NL9
100.00	CB7	31		Cash							
		31		Balance c/d		100.00					
						158.00					
		Mar 1		Balance b/d							

Fig. 24. Example of a completed page in a petty cash book.

15 How to write up the petty cash book—cont.

Step-by-step

1. Enter in the third column the date that the fund or float was received.

2. Write in the fourth ('particulars') column the word 'cash' or 'bank' as appropriate, depending on whether the float came from the cashier by cash, or from the bank by cheque.

3. Write the imprest amount in the first column (debit cash column). Unless the system is being started from scratch, this stage will have been completed previously. The procedure for all other entries will start from step 4 below.

4. Record from each cash invoice the date, purchase invoice number, purpose of expenditure, gross and net invoice total and VAT, as shown on the page opposite. Enter the net total directly into a suitable analysis column.

5. Whenever necessary (end of period, end of page) total up the two main columns. The cashier should reimburse the petty cash fund for what has been spent, to restore the fund to its original imprest figure. Then balance the two columns, just like any other ledger account: entering a balancing item (the difference between the two totals) to make each side add up to the same amount. That balancing item should be annotated 'balance c/d' (carried down). The counterpart of that balancing item should then be recorded after the totals as the *opening* figure for the *next* period and annotated 'balance b/d' (brought down).

6. Next, total up each analysis column and the VAT column and cross check with the gross invoice total column, to make sure there are no mistakes.

Entering the folio references
Enter folio references for the debit side in the folio column, *eg* CB (cash book)7. Enter those relating to the credit side at the foot of their respective column totals: it is only the *totals* that will be posted to the Ledger, e.g. travelling expenses, folio reference NL6 (Nominal Ledger item 6) in the example opposite.

THE JOURNAL

Date	Particulars	Fo.	Dr.	Cr.
200X				
Feb 20	Morgan and Baldwyn	SL15	25.00	
	Sales	NL1		25.00
	To correct error of original entry			
21	Drawings	PL3	70.00	
	Purchases	NL6		70.00
	To record goods taken from stock for private use			
22	Sundries:			
	Motor Van 2	NL39	8,000.00	
	Edwards Garage	BL16		8,000.00
	Asset Disposal A/C	NL40	3,350.00	
	Motor Van 1	NL10		3,350.00
	Edwards Garage	BL16	2,000.00	
	Asset Disposal A/C	NL40		2,000.00
	Profit and Loss A/C	NL41	1,350.00	
	Asset Disposal A/C	NL40		1,350.00
	Edwards Garage	BL16	6,000.00	
	Bank	CB18		6,000.00
	To record the details of the purchase by cheque of a motorvan with part exchange on old motor van.			

Fig. 25. Example of a complete page of Journal entry. Note: You would normally expect provision for depreciation account to also feature in such a combination entry as this, but here it does not in the interests of simplicity.

16 The journal

A general purpose record

A book of prime entry, the journal is simply a place for making the first record of any transaction for which no other prime entry book is suitable. It has debit and credit columns, but they are simpler than those of the cash book and petty cash book. The journal itself is not part of the accounts, merely one of the sources from which the accounts are written up later on.

Examples of journal entries

Here are some examples of transactions you would need the journal to record:

- opening figures of a new business (e.g. list of assets)
- bad debts
- depreciation (e.g. of vehicles or equipment)
- purchase and sales of fixed assets (e.g. vehicles or plant)
- correction of errors
- goods taken for private use (as against for sale)
- ledger transfer needed if a book debt were sold.

Information needed for an entry

When entering a transaction into the journal, you need to record these aspects of it:

- date
- accounts affected
- folio references
- amounts (debit and credit)
- reason.

Write a brief explanation against each entry. Separate each new entry from the one above by ruling a horizontal line right across the page (see page 42).

Sometimes it is a good idea to make combination double entries, i.e. where there is more than one debit entry per credit entry, or vice versa. This would be appropriate when journalising 'opening figures', which include various assets and liabilities, together with the capital figure to which they relate. A group of entries are recorded on the opposite page with the prefix 'Sundries', which all relate to trading in an old motor van for a new one.

On the next page we will see how to write up the journal step-by-step.

THE JOURNAL

Date	Particulars	Fo.	Dr.	Cr.
200X				
May 28	L. Cleese	SL6	60.00	
	L. Cleaves	SL10		60.00
	To correct error			
	of commission			
30	Profit & Loss A/C	NL30	85.00	
	F. Evans	SL8		85.00
	To write off bad debt			

Fig. 26. Journalising an item in the sales ledger.

1. Journalise the following:
On 28 May 200X it is discovered that L. Cleaves' a/c in the sales ledger has wrongly been debited with the sum of £60. Such sum should have been debited to L. Cleese's a/c instead. Two days later, F. Evans, a debtor of the firm, is declared bankrupt and the firm expects no ultimate settlement of his a/c in the sum of £85.00.

2. Using the following information, calculate the capital, journalise the opening figures and post them to the ledger for A. Frazer, a retail stationer, who started business on 1 April 200X. Cash at bank £1,450.00, cash in hand £50.00, office equipment £1,500.00, land and buildings £54,000, fixtures and fittings £4,000.00, a motor van £3,000.00 and stock £2,000.

THE JOURNAL

Date	Particulars	Fo.	Dr.	Cr.
200X				
	Sundries			
Apr 1	Land and buildings	NL1	54,000.00	
	Fixtures & fittings	NL2	4,000.00	
	Office equipment	NL3	1,500.00	
	Motor van	NL4	3,000.00	
	Stock	NL5	2,000.00	
	Cash at bank	CB1	1,450.00	
	Cash in hand	CB1	50.00	
	Capital	NL6		66,000.00
	To record opening figures			

Fig. 27. Journalising the opening figures.

17   How to write up the journal

Using miscellaneous source documents

There are no routine source documents for this job, as there are for example for the purchase day book (purchase invoices) or for the cash book (cheque counterfoils etc). The journal is a miscellany, and its sources will be miscellaneous. They may be documented by nothing more than a rough note, if indeed they are documented at all. For example, the sales manager may pass a memo to the journal clerk saying that a customer has gone into liquidation, so that its debt to the firm will have to be written off. Similarly a roughly pencilled note from the accountant, saying what depreciation should apply to an asset, may be your only source document for an entry.

Writing up the journal step-by-step

1. Enter the date in column one (the date column).

2. Enter the names of the ledger accounts which will be affected by this entry, e.g. Motor Van Account, or Profit & Loss Account, as in example 1 opposite. Indent the credit entry (usually the second entry). The folio column gives the 'address' of the account in question in the ledger, for example NL (nominal ledger), CB (cash book), PCB (petty cash book) and SL (sales ledger).

3. Record the amounts against each ledger account name. Note: these last two steps provide the posting instructions for the ledger clerk. Many debit entries may have a common credit entry, as with opening figures. If so, prefix them with the word 'sundries'.

4. Explain, briefly but precisely, your reason for the entry, e.g. 'To write off bad debt' or 'To record opening figures'.

5. When you have finished, underline the entry right across the page.

POSTAGE BOOK

Dr.	Date 200X	Particulars	Cr. £ p
92.00	Jan 1	Balance b/d	
	1	Edwards	20
	1	Bandura	26
	1	Jones	26
	1	Northern Electricity	1.30
	1	J.B.C. Roofing	20
	1	Evans	20
	4	Eliot Transport	26
	4	Morgan and Baldwin	26
	5	Entwhistle	2.60
	9	Davidson	26
	10	A.T. Office Supplies	20
	15	Baker	26
	25	Cleaves	26
	25	Gange	26
	25	Entwhistle	26
	28	Keele Engineering	20
	29	Razi and Thaung	2.60
	29	Eliot Transport	20
	29	Inko	20
	30	Kahn and Kahn	26
	31	Keele Engineering	1.30
	31	Evans	20
	31	Jones	20
	31	Baker	20
	31	Edwards	20
12.60	31	11 × 20p + 40 x 26p	
	31	Balance b/d	92.00
104.60			104.60
92.00	Feb 1	Balance c/d	

Fig. 28. Example of a postage book page.

18 The postage book

This book is like the petty cash book, in that it is a subsidiary account book. It gives a useful record of a fund entrusted to an employee, in this case the postage clerk. This person may have several other junior jobs to do within the office, such as reception/telephonist.

The postage book works much like the petty cash book, except that there is no VAT to deal with, and no analysis columns. It, too, is run on an imprest system, whereby the fund is topped up from time to time to its original level (the imprest amount).

One big difference, however, is that the fund is not kept as notes and coins: cash received by the postage clerk is used immediately to buy postage stamps. The fund exists in the form of stamps, not cash.

It differs even more from the petty cash book, and indeed from any of the other books, because it is not even a book of prime entry, providing sources for ledger posting. So it is really on the edges of the accounting system. The real source of postage data for the ledger is the cash book: this records cash paid into the postage fund.

Nevertheless, it is a useful financial record for the firm. It provides details of a current asset (even if small) in the form of postage stamps; it is the only source document from which this detail can be gleaned. The postage book also provides a record of the financial relationship between the postage clerk and the firm.

You can buy books specifically designed for this purpose, though any general notebook with cash columns can be ruled up to do the job.

Writing up the postage book step-by-step
You will need:
- the receipt slips for stamps purchased (supplied by the Post Office)
- the stamped letters and/or parcels to be sent out.

Suppose the imprest amount was £92.00.

1. Record the date in the date column, with year/month to start.
2. Record the combined value of any stamps purchased, from the receipt slips, in the first (debit cash) column. In the third ('particulars') column record the breakdown of the stamps purchased, e.g. 11 x 20p and 40 x 26p as in the example opposite.
3. List the addressees' names shown on the envelopes or parcels, in the third column ('particulars'), recording against each in the fourth (credit cash) column the value of the stamps affixed.
4. When desired, the cashier can be asked to replenish the fund to the original imprest amount of £92.00. At such times the two columns should be totalled, treating the imprest figure as the balancing item.

SALES DAY BOOK

Date	Supplier	Inv. No.	Net. Inv Value	Stationery	Books
200X					
Feb 4	S. Jones	2/1	200.00	200.00	

CASH BOOK

CB10

Date 200X	Particulars	Fo.	Discount	Cash	Bank	Date 200X	Particulars	Fo.	Discount	Cash	Bank
Feb 1	Balance	b/d			9,000.00	Feb 1	Petty Cash	PC15			50.00
28	S.Jones	SL17	10.00		190.00	28	Balance	c/d			9,140.00
			10.00		9,190.00						9,190.00
Mar 1	Balance	b/d			9,140.00						

PETTY CASH BOOK

P15

Receipts	Fo.	Date	Details	Rec	Total Exp.	Motor Exp.	Trvlng
		200X					
50.00	CB10	Feb 1	Cash				
		1	Petrol	5/1	10.00	10.00	
		28	Balance c/d		40.00		
50.00					50.00	10.00	
40.00		Mar 1	Balance b/d			NL9	

JOURNAL

Date	Particulars	Fo.	Dr.	Cr.
200X				
Feb 21	Drawings	PL3	70.00	
	Purchases	NL6		70.00
	To record goods taken for private use			

Fig. 29. Examples of entries in books of prime entry to be posted to the ledger (see page 52).

19   The ledger

The firm's official record

The ledger is the 'official' record of a firm's accounts. We sometimes speak of the general ledger, the bought ledger, sales ledger and cash book separately—as if they were separate 'ledgers'. But to an accountant the ledger is a single unit, even if it is made up of physically separate books. The ledger is really a 'system' rather than a book. Whatever form it takes—books or computer disks etc—'the ledger' means the master record of all the firm's financial affairs.

Divisions of the ledger

We have already discovered two parts of the ledger—the cash book and the petty cash book—which also happen to be books of prime entry. The only difference in the ruling between that and the other divisions we will now deal with is that the latter are simpler. The cash book has three cash columns on each side; the other divisions of the ledger have only one. (However where ledger posting is done on a computer the format involves three columns, a debit and credit column and a running balance column. This is because the running balance can easily be calculated electronically—it doesn't call on the time and effort of the book-keeper. In manual systems, working out such running balances is considered a waste of time.)

The other ledger divisions are:

- the general ledger (often called the nominal ledger)

- the personal ledger, subdivided into bought ledger (or purchase ledger) and sales ledger (or debtors ledger)

- a private ledger is sometimes kept, in which capital items are posted, for example proprietor's drawings. It is sometimes kept away from staff because the proprietor considers such information confidential.

The nominal and personal ledger

In the nominal ledger the impersonal aspects of transactions are posted, for example purchases, sales figures, wages, stationery and asset purchases. In the personal ledger the personal side of each transaction is posted, i.e. the credit to suppliers' accounts when the firm has purchased something, and the debit to customers' accounts when the firm has sold something.

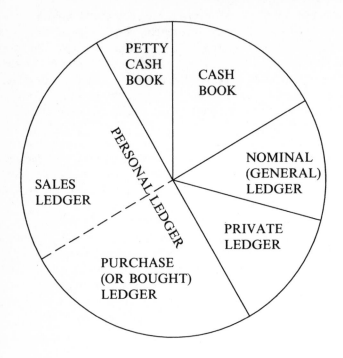

Fig. 30. The ledger.

Different accounts within the ledger

Each part of the ledger contains a number of different accounts—one for each expense item, revenue asset or liability, as they will appear in the final accounts. For example, there will be an account for purchases, an account for sales, an account for wages, and a separate account for each asset such as Motor Car 1 account, Motor Car 2 account or Printing Machine account, and so on.

A variety of forms

Though the ruling of each type of book is reasonably standard, both the ledger and books of prime entry are found in a variety of forms. Indeed, they don't have to be 'books' at all. They can be sheets of analysis paper in a loose leaf binder, or written into a computer program so that the rulings appear on a VDU screen. Entries are then made via the keyboard rather than with pen and paper.

In a looseleaf ledger system these divisions (sales, purchases, nominal etc) may take the form of cardboard page dividers. If bound books are used, each division may be a physically separate bound book. The personal ledger (purchase ledger/sales ledger) will contain a separate account for each supplier and customer. The arrangement of accounts in each division is flexible.

Post only from books of prime entry

Nothing should ever be posted into the ledger except from the books of prime entry.

Never, for example, post information into the ledger directly from such things as invoices, bank statements, cheque counterfoils, petty cash receipt slips and so on. These are source documents for the books of prime entry.

Recording each transaction twice

We have already seen how each transaction in double entry book-keeping has two aspects—a debit and a credit. So each transaction has to be recorded in two separate places, on the debit side and on the credit side. It follows that at any moment in time the total number of debit entries must exactly equal the total of credit entries (unless a mistake has been made). In a small office, one ledger clerk will probably handle all the divisions (except perhaps the cash book). In a large firm there may be a separate bought ledger clerk, sales ledger clerk, and so on.

SALES LEDGER

p17							
			S. Jones				
			200X				
Feb 4	Sales	NL7	200.00	Feb 28	Bank	CB10	190.00
				28	Discount allowed	NL8	10.00
			235.00				200.00

NOMINAL LEDGER

p6			
	Purchases		
	200X		
	Feb 21	Drawings	PL3	70.00

p7			
	Sales		
	200X		
	Feb 4	S. Jones	SL17	200.00

p8		
	Discount Allowed	
200X		
Feb 28 S. Jones	SL17	10.00

p9		
	Motor Expenses	
200X		
Feb 1 Petty Cash	PC15	10.00

PRIVATE LEDGER

p3		
	Drawings	
200X		
Feb 21 Purchases NL6		70.00

Fig. 31. Postings to the ledger from the prime entries on page 48.

52

20   Posting to the ledger from the day books

What you will need
- The ledger in all its parts—all the books or sheets that make up the complete ledger or at least the part you are concerned with, e.g. the purchase ledger.
- All the books of prime entry, or those you are concerned with, e.g. the purchase day book.

Posting from the purchase day book to the ledger
1. Turn to the start of the entries in the purchase day book as yet unposted to the ledger. Your first job is to post each purchase invoice (gross) to the credit of the supplier concerned, in his personal ledger account. The personal ledger should have an index of supplier's names, telling you on what page in the ledger you will find their account. (If no account exists, you will need to open one. Just head a new page with the supplier's name, and remember to list it in the index.)
2. In the first (date) column, write the date of entry.
3. Write the name of the account to which the other side of the transaction will be posted, in column 2 ('particulars').
4. In the fourth (cash) column record the gross value, in other words including VAT, of the transaction.
5. Now make the dual aspect of these postings: post the column totals for the net amount (i.e. net goods value) and VAT, to the debit of purchases and VAT accounts respectively. The procedure is the same as for posting the personal side of the transaction, following steps 1 to 4.

Posting from the purchase returns day book to the ledger
This is the reverse of posting from the purchase day book. This time you debit personal accounts in the bought ledger, and credit the VAT account and a purchase returns account in the nominal ledger.

Posting from the sales day book
This is just like posting from the purchase day book, except that you debit personal accounts in the sales ledger, and credit the VAT account and a sales account in the nominal ledger.

Posting from the sales returns day book
This is the reverse of posting from the sales day book: you credit personal accounts in the sales ledger, and debit the VAT account and a sales account in the nominal ledger.

Dr.					A. T. Office Supplies			Cr.
200X					200X			
					May 1	Balance	c/d	380.00
					26	Purchases	NL9	620.00
May	28	Bank	CB17	380.00				
	31	Balance	c/d	620.00				
				1,000.00				1,000.00
					Jun 1	Balance	b/d	620.00

Fig. 32. Postings to the purchase ledger.

1. Postings to the purchase ledger

Suppose that, as at the last day of April 200X, A. Frazer owed A. T. Office Supplies the sum of £380.00. On the 26 May the firm purchased further goods from A. T. Office Supplies for £620. On 28 May the firm paid its April statement by cheque. This is what the ledger postings would look like (*and remember, they have to be recorded in the books of prime entry first*).

2. Postings to the sales ledger

Suppose that K. Gange is a customer of A. Frazer, and at the close of last month (January 200X) his a/c balance stood at £2,100.00. Suppose that on 4 February Gange returned goods to the value of £100.00. On 6 February Gange purchased a further £1,000 worth of goods. On 12 February he paid his January a/c, after deducting the returned goods and a 2½% agreed discount for payment within 14 days. Gange then purchased a further £980.00 worth of goods on 18 February and then £220.00 worth of goods on 26 February. This is what the ledger postings would look like:

Dr.					K. Gange			Cr.
200X					200X			
Feb	1	Balance	b/d	2,100.00	Feb 4	Sales Rtrns	NL19	100.00
	6	Sales	NL18	1,000.00				
					12	Bank	CB6	1,950.00
	18	Sales	NL18	980.00	12	Discount allowed	NL22	50.00
	26	Sales	NL18	220.00	28	Balance	c/d	2,200.00
				4,300.00				4,300.00
Mar	1	Balance	b/d	2,200.00				

Fig. 33. Postings to the sales ledger.

21   Posting to the ledger from the cash book

The cash book entries are, by their very nature, one side of the double entry. All you have to do now is to make the other side of the entry:

Step-by-step
1. Every time you post in the cash book, make an opposite posting to the relevant personal account in the bought or sales ledger as appropriate. The narration against each of these postings will be 'cash' (if the payment was in the cash column of the cash book) or 'bank' (if it was in the bank column). Now you have to post any discounts from the discounts column. Remember, although the cash book is part of the ledger, this column does not have such status; it is a single entry element sitting inside a ledger division, while not exactly being part of it. So the postings from the discounts column must be twofold, just as for any other prime entry source.

2. Post the discounts to the correct personal accounts, making sure they are to the opposite sides to the ones on which they appear in the cash book.

3. Post the column totals to the other side of the 'Discount allowed' or 'Discount received' accounts in the nominal ledger as applicable, to complete your dual posting. Use the name of the account to which the dual posting has gone for this purpose in all ledger posting.

Posting from the petty cash book
The petty cash book may, or may not, be treated as part of the double entry system. If it is, as with the cash book, its entries will themselves already contain one side of the ledger posting; you have only to make the other. However, this one aspect of the dual entry is itself split into various postings to nominal ledger accounts and this is why analysis columns have been used. Their individual totals, together with the VAT column total, provide the figures to be posted to the various accounts denoted by their column headings. The net invoice total column is not posted anywhere.

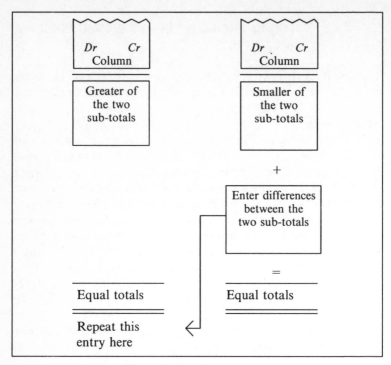

Fig. 34. Balancing the ledger.

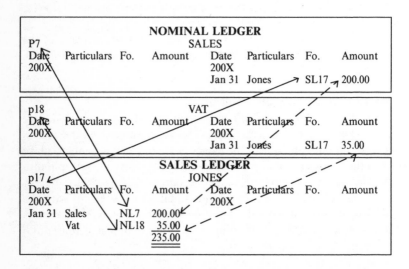

Fig. 35. In the above examples of Folio Column entry you will see that each posting is cross-referenced with another. Note also that the Sales Ledger should not be confused with the 'Sales A/C' in the Nominal Ledger.

22 Balancing the ledger

Periodically, usually once a month, the ledger accounts are balanced.

Balancing the ledger step-by-step

1. Total up both the debit and credit sides individually. Work out what figure you need to add to the lower figure to equalise the totals. Write against this figure: 'Balance c/d' (carried down).
2. Rule off. Enter the two equal totals and underline twice, to show they are final totals.
3. Enter the same figure on the opposite side below the total box: this will be the opening figure for the new period. Write against it: 'Balance b/d' (brought down). Note: you do not need to do this if the account only contains one item; in such a case no lines are drawn, and no dual totals entered.

The word 'balances' as used here simply means differences.

Completing the folio columns

We have now posted all our entries to the ledger. The next stage before extracting the trial balance is to complete the folio columns against each posting in the ledger. These columns show the ledger 'address' (ledger division and page number) where the counterpart posting has been made. Let's take as an example the folio column beside a posting in the sales account of the nominal ledger; we might perhaps write 'SL8' for the address of a personal account in the sales ledger, i.e. it is on sales ledger page 8. The name of the account in which the counterpart posting has been made is entered in the particulars column of each ledger account, so you could say that this extra cross-referencing is unnecessary. But if the ledger divisions are large, a note of the exact page number could save time. Also filling in the folio columns will help the detection of errors. If the trial balance fails, errors of omission can be spotted by the absence of a folio column posting, because it could mean that no counterpart posting has been made.

Important points to understand

Of all the things students find difficult to grasp in book-keeping, two in particular stand out.

- The first is knowing whether to debit or credit an account. Which is the debit aspect and which the credit aspect of the transaction? What does it really mean to debit or credit an account?
- The second is knowing which nominal ledger accounts to post the impersonal side of transactions to, i.e.: knowing how to classify expenses and revenues into the right account names in the first place.

22 Balancing the ledger—cont.

As for how to name the overhead Expense a/cs, with the exception of limited companies (whose final accounts formats are governed by law—see p.122) there is no hard and fast rule. Each firm and each accountancy practice will have defined its own range. The various worked examples of trial balances in this book will give you some idea. The range of asset and liability account names are a little easier to suggest, since the anticipated balance sheet effectively governs the range of accounts which will be set up. There is a good degree of consistency between firms in this respect and the range which tends to be used can be memorised in terms of 4 levels of classification.

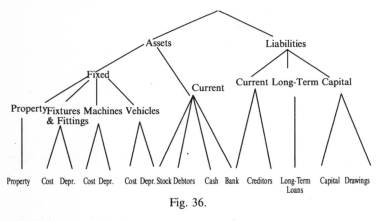

Fig. 36.

You will see that this classification gives us an eventual 15 asset/liability accounts, but there may be more, e.g.: if the firm has more than one machine there will be a separate asset and depreciation account for each of them.

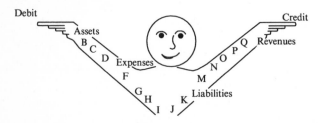

Fig. 37. Let Alf Direct You.

Once you have mastered how to categorise things into assets, expenses, liabilities and revenues then with this simple model in memory you cannot go wrong.

Taking the first point first:

1.   The word debit comes from the Latin verb *debere*, meaning 'to owe'; debit is the Latin for he or she owes. In business, a person owes to the proprietor that which was loaned or given to him by the proprietor.

2.   The word credit comes from the Latin verb *credere*, meaning 'to trust' or 'to believe'. Our creditors believe in our integrity, and trust us to pay them for goods and services they supply; so they are willing to deliver them without asking for immediate payment.

Perhaps this will help a little in personal ledger accounts; but what about the impersonal accounts of the nominal ledger? Whenever an account has a debit balance it means that it 'owes' the proprietor the value of it (and vice versa for credit balances), as if that account were a person.

```
┌─────────────────────────────────────────────────────────┐
│            RED HOUSE CEMENT WORKS                        │
│               Mulvy Island Road                          │
│               Anytown, Anyshire.                         │
│                                                          │
│  Invoice No:-              002345                        │
│                                         £      p         │
│  100 Bags of cement @ £10            1,000.00            │
│  Less 35% Trade Discount               350.00           │
│                                        650.00            │
│  Plus VAT                              113.75            │
│  Total                                 763.75            │
│                                                          │
│  Terms strictly 30 days net                             │
└─────────────────────────────────────────────────────────┘
```

Fig. 38. Example of the way trade discount may be shown on
a wholesaler's invoice to a retailer.

```
┌─────────────────────────────────────────────────────────┐
│    S. JONES (WHOLESALE STATIONERY SUPPLIES) LTD         │
│         210 Barton High Street, Barton, Barshire        │
│                                                          │
│    Invoice No: 00322               10/2/200X            │
│                                                          │
│    10 reams of typing paper @ £7        70.00           │
│    plus VAT        17½%                 12.25           │
│                                         82.25           │
│                                                          │
│    2½% early settlement discount                        │
│    Deduct £2.06 if paid within                          │
│    14 days.                                              │
│                                                          │
│    ┌                    ┐                                │
│    │ Customer                                            │
│    │ Razi & Thaung                                       │
│    │ 15 Bolton Road                                      │
│    │ Finchester        ┘                                 │
└─────────────────────────────────────────────────────────┘
```

Fig. 39. Example of the way early settlement discount may be shown on an
invoice.

23 Discounts

Trade discounts

A trade discount is one given by wholesalers to retailers, so that the retailers can make a profit on the price at which they sell goods to the public. Example:

Wholesale price of 5 litre tin of paint:	£4.00
Trade discount:	£2.00
Recommended retail price:	£6.00

In this example, the trade discount is $33^1/_3$ of the recommended retail price. However, trade discounts have no place as such in a firm's accounts. They are deducted before any entry is made in any of the books. As far as the wholesaler is concerned, his price to the retailer is simply £4.00, so £4.00 is the amount the wholesaler enters in his sales day book, and the amount the retailer enters in his purchase day book.

Early settlement discounts

These are discounts offered to persuade customers to settle their debts to the firm early. Typically, a discount of $2\frac{1}{2}\%$ might be offered for payment within 14 days. But the details can vary. Example:

Building materials supplied:	£200.00
Less 2% discount for settlement within 7 days:	£ 4.00
	£196.00

Firms offer such discounts for two reasons: to speed up cash flow and to reduce the chance of debts becoming bad debts (the longer a debt remains outstanding, the more likely it is to become a bad debt).

If you write up your day books daily, you will not know whether or not an early settlement discount will be taken. You will know once the actual payment arrives. So you have to enter the figure without any deduction of discount into your sales day book. When the debt is paid, if a discount has been properly claimed, the credit entry to that customer's account will be $2\frac{1}{2}\%$ less than the account shows. You then need to enter the discount as a credit to his account and a debit to 'discount allowed account' in the nominal ledger. This will make up the shortfall. It has the same effect as cash on the customer's personal account—and so it should: the offer shown on the invoice is like a 'money off voucher', and we would expect to treat that the same as cash.

Discounts and VAT

An early settlement discount is based on the invoice total (including VAT). Whether it is claimed or not will not alter the net sale value or the VAT amount which will be entered in the books.

CASH BOOK

Dr.   **Cr.**

Date 200X	Particulars	Fo.	Discount	Cash	Bank	Date 200X	Particulars	Fo.	Discount	Cash	Bank
Mar 1	Balance	b/d		50.00	1,000.00	Mar 13	Eliot		7.64		297.81
13	Morgan & Baldwyn	SL5	13.71		260.34						
20	Edwards' Garage	SL7			193.40						
28	A. Singh	SL9			640.39	31	Balance	c/d		50.00	1,796.32
			13.71	50.00	2,094.13				7.64	50.00	2,094.13
Aprl 1	Balance b/d			50.00	1,796.32						

PURCHASE LEDGER

BL3

Dr.   *Eliot Transport*   **Cr.**

200X					200X			
					Mar 1	Balance b/d		305.45
Mar 10	Bank	CB8	297.81					
10	Disc recd	NL19	7.64					
			305.45					305.45

SALES LEDGER

SL9

Dr.   *A. Singh*   **Cr.**

200X				200X			
Mar 1	Balance	b/d	674.10	Mar 1	Bank	CB8	640.39
				31	Balance	c/d	33.71
			674.10				674.10

SL18

Dr.   *Edwards Garage*   **Cr.**

200X				200X		
Mar 1	Balance	b/d	193.40	Mar 20	Bank	193.40

SL20

Dr.   *Morgan and Baldwin*   **Cr.**

200X				200X			
Mar 1	Balance	b/d	274.05	Mar 13	Bank	CB8	260.34
				13	Discount All	NL18	13.71
			274.05				274.05

NOMINAL LEDGER

NL18

Dr.   *Discounts Allowed*   **Cr.**

200X			200X
Mar 31	Debtors	13.71	

NL19

Dr.   *Discounts Received*   **Cr.**

200X		200X		
		Mar 31	Creditors	7.64

Fig. 40. Recording discounts in cash book and ledger.

23   Discounts—cont.

Prime entry of discounts in the cash book

You make your prime entry of discounts in the cash book. But the column you use is unlike the other cash columns: it is not a ledger column, just a prime entry 'lodging place'. Entries in the discount column of the cash book, unlike entries in its other (ledger) columns, are not part of a dual posting; the dual posting is made in the 'discount allowed account' in the nominal ledger for the one part, and the personal customer account in the sales ledger for the other (or 'discounts received account' and supplier account, as the case may be). The postings to the discount accounts in the nominal ledger are, of course, column totals rather than individual items.

Entering early settlement discounts

Both the cashier and the ledger clerk will be involved in entering early settlement discounts. When the cheques are first received from customers or sent out to suppliers the cashier will check whether they have been properly claimed by reference to the time limit for early settlement discount and then enter the discounts in the cash book when he is entering the other payment details. For this step-by-step process please refer to pages 25 and 27.

At the end of each month the ledger clerk will make the dual postings to the ledger accounts for each item in the discount columns of the cash book.

Step-by-step

What you will need is the cash book, sales ledger, purchase ledger and nominal ledger.

1. One by one, post each item in the Discounts Received column to the debit of the named suppliers' purchase ledger accounts.

2. Post the column total for the month to the credit of Discounts Received a/c in the nominal ledger.

3. One by one, post each item in the Discounts Allowed column to the credit of the named customers' sales ledger Accounts.

4. Post the column totals to the debit of Discounts Allowed a/c in the nominal ledger.

SALES LEDGER

Total Debtors Account

Dr.						Cr.
Balance	b/d	200.00	Cheques			150.00
Sales		300.00	Balance		c/d	350.00
		500.00				500.00

Fig. 41. An example of a total debtors acount.

PURCHASE LEDGER

Total Creditors Account

Dr.						Cr.
Cash Paid to			Balance		b/d	2,000.00
Suppliers		1,200.00	Purchases			2,200.00
Balance	c/d	3,000.00				
		4,200.00				4,200.00

Fig. 42. An example of a total creditors account.

SALES LEDGER
Sales Ledger Control Account

200X					200X				
Feb	1	Balance	b/d	15,000	Feb	28	Sales Returns		200
	28	Sales		10,000		28	Bank		11,100
						28	Discounts Allowed		400
						28	Bad Debts		300
						28	Balance	c/d	13,000
				25,000					25,000
Mar	1	Balance	b/d	13,000					

Fig. 43. Example of a more complex sales ledger control account.

24 Control accounts

Useful summaries
A control account is a sort of trial balance for just one ledger division. You write the account at the back of the ledger division concerned. The main idea of control accounts is to subdivide the task of the main trial balance. They also provide useful summaries of data for more effective financial management. For example the boss might want an up-to-date figure for total debtors, to help him monitor credit control in the firm. Control accounts are in fact sometimes called total accounts (for example, total creditors account).

Subdividing the work
In a small firm, where one book-keeper posts all the ledgers, control accounts might be unnecessary. But the double entry system can be quickly expanded if necessary by using control acounts. Individual specialist book-keepers, such as the bought ledger clerk or sales ledger clerk, could balance their own ledger division using a control total, i.e. a balancing item equal to the difference between all their own debit and credit balances. A head book-keeper could then build up an overall trial balance just by taking the control account totals. In large firms today, control accounts are vital to the smooth running of the accounting system. Without them, reaching a trial balance would really be a difficult, time-consuming and messy business.

Source documents for control accounts
The source documents you need for posting to control accounts are the books of prime entry. But you only need monthly (or other period) totals, not individual entries as with other postings. Each entry in the sales day book, for example, you post separately to a specific account in the sales ledger, but you only post the total of gross invoice values to the sales ledger control account.

The four day books for sales and purchases are well suited to control accounts; column totals are readily available. It may be a good idea to add a gross invoice total column if control accounts are going to be kept. The other day books are not quite so helpful in this respect, since they do not analyse totals of different classes. Take the cash book, for example. From here you take the total of payments to suppliers, but 'purchases' may be mixed up with 'expenses' such as drawings, wages, transfers to petty cash, and other types of payments, all of which must be totalled up for posting to control accounts. Still, while not being quite so easy as posting from the sales and purchase day books, it is not too difficult to use the cash book for control accounts.

Dr.					Sales Ledger Control			Cr.
200X					200X			
Sep	30	Balance	b/d	20,263.60	Oct	31	Sales Returns	500.00
Oct	31	Sales		24,630.70		31	Cheques	22,840.90
						31	Disc. Alld.	250.80
						31	Bad Debts	420.50
						31	Balance c/d	20,882.10
				44,894.30				44,894.30
Nov	1	Balance	b/d	20,882.10				

Fig. 44. A. Frazer's sales ledger control account.

1. Suppose:
The balance of A. Frazer's sales ledger control account as at the end of September 200X was £20,263.60 Dr.

   Total sales for the month of October 200X were £24,630.70.
   Total payments received for the month were £22,840.90.
   Total discounts allowed for the month were £250.80.
   Total bad debts written off for the month were £420.50.
   Total Sales Returns were £500.00.

Write up the sales ledger control account for October 200X.

2. Suppose:
The balance of A. Frazer's purchase ledger control account as at 31 August 200X was £1,293.00 Cr.
   Total purchases during September 200X amounted to £18,950.
   Total payments to creditors were £9,800.00.
   Total discounts received were £250.

Write up the purchase ledger control account for the month of September 200X.

Dr.					Purchase Ledger Control			Cr.
200X					200X			
Sept	30	Cheques		9,800.00	Aug	31	Balance b/d	1,293.00
	30	Disc. Rec.		250.00	Sept	30	Purchases	18,950.00
	30	Balance	c/d	10,193.00				
				20,243.00				20,243.00
					Oct	1	Balance b/d	10,193.00

Fig. 45. A. Frazer's purchase ledger control account.

25 Preparing control accounts step-by-step

What you need

- the ledger (or those parts of it for which you want to operate control accounts)

- the relevant day books.

Step-by-step

1. Unless the control account is a new one, your opening balances will already be there. These are merely the closing balances for the previous month. If the control account is created at the start of a year, you can take your opening balances of assets and liabilities from the trial balance.

2. Take each of the four day books relating to sales and purchases. Post the monthly gross invoice (or credit note) totals to the sales or purchase ledger control account as the case may be. Post the totals to the same side as the individual postings were made, i.e. debit customers accounts for sales, and so on. Annotate each posting accordingly, for example 'sales', 'sales returns' and so on.

3. Take each of the other books of prime entry, and extract from them totals for all the classes of transaction that relate to the ledger divisions concerned. Post each of these in turn to the relevant control acounts. Again, the appropriate side is exactly the same you would use if you were posting the items individually. Annotate each posting accordingly, for example 'cash', 'bank' and so on.

4. Total up and balance each control account as you would any other ledger account.

Note on purchase and sales ledger control accounts

The purchase and sales ledger control accounts can be treated as part of the double entry system, but if they are the individual personal accounts in the purchase and sales ledgers must not be; they must simply be treated as an analysis. One or the other can be included in the double entry system—not both.

ARMSTRONG ENGINEERING
Trial Balance as at 31 March 200X

Ledger balances

Sales		100,000
Fixtures and fittings	15,000	
Freehold Premises	40,000	
Motor Van	8,000	
Debtors	10,000	
Stock (opening)	10,000	
Cash at bank	10,000	
Cash in hand	50	
Capital		63,050
Bad Debts	2,000	
Bad Debts Provision		2,000
Drawings	6,450	
Depreciation	2,350	
Provision for Depreciation on Motor Van		1,600
Provision for Depreciation on Fixtures and Fittings		750
Purchases	60,000	
Motor Expenses	750	
Heat and Light	800	
Wages	10,000	
Postage and Stationery	550	
Repairs and Renewals	250	
Creditors		12,000
Interest and Banking Charges	200	
Carriage	3,000	
Closing Stock	9,000	9,000
	188,400	= 188,400
	(debit balances)	= *(credit balances)*

Fig. 46. A typical trial balance, listing all the debit and credit balances in the ledger.

26　The trial balance

A listing of ledger balances

The trial balance is unlike anything we have seen so far, but it is quite simple to understand and quite simple to do. It is just a listing of all the ledger balances at a particular moment in time. You list the balances in two columns—one for the debit balances and one for the credit balances. If all the ledger divisions have been correctly posted your two columns will balance. Remember, for every transaction there have been two postings, a debit and a credit, so the sum of all the debits should equal the sum of all the credits. See example opposite.

We always talk of 'extracting' a trial balance, or 'constructing' or 'drawing up' a trial balance.

Summary

The trial balance is:

- a way of checking the accuracy of all previous postings

- a source, in a useful summary form, for putting together the firm's final accounts later on.

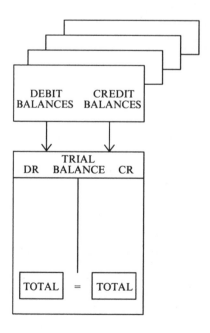

Trial Balance: A. Frazer & Co

	Dr.	Cr.
Purchases	28,879.00	
Sales		48,133.00
Bank	981.00	
Cash	50.00	
Land and Buildings	490,000.00	
Machinery	100,000.00	
Fixtures and fittings	60,000.00	
Motor Vehicle	80,000.00	
Stock	3,600.00	
Debtors	2,010.00	
Creditors		3,190.00
Opening Capital		178,199.00
Long-term, secured loan creditor		548,031.00
Heat and light	400.00	
Motoring Expenses	1,480.00	
Insurance	240.00	
Wages	6,913.00	
Salaries	3,000.00	
	777,553.00	777,553.00

Fig. 47. Worked example of a trial balance. Note: there will be pence as well as pounds in a real life trial balance, but we have omitted them to keep things simple.

Suppose the ledger balances of A. Frazer for the month of August 200X were as follows:

Purchases, £28, 879.00 Dr, Sales £48,133.00 Cr, Bank £981.00 Dr, Cash £50.00 Dr, Land and Buildings £490,000.00 Dr, Machinery £100,000 Dr, Motor vehicle £80,000.00 Dr, Fixtures and fittings £60,000 Dr, Stock £3,600.00 Dr, Debtors £2,010.00 Dr, Creditors £3,190.00 Cr, Opening Capital £178,199 Cr, Long-term, secured loan creditor £548,031.00 Cr, Heat and light £400.00 Dr, Motoring Expenses £1,480.00 Dr, Insurance £240.00 Dr, Wages £6,913.00 Dr, Salaries £3,000.00 Dr.

Construct a trial balance as at 31 August 200X.

27   How to extract a trial balance

What you need
- the ledger (including of course the cash book and petty cash book, which are both part of the ledger)
- a sheet of A4 paper.

Preparation
Make sure that all the folio columns have been entered in all the ledger accounts. Enter them now if necessary.

Extracting a trial balance step-by-step
1. Head your blank sheet 'Trial balance as at [date]'. Rule two cash columns down the right hand side. Head them, 'Debit' and 'Credit'.
2. List the balances of every single ledger account, including the cash book and petty cash book. Put each one in the correct column of your trial balance (debit, or credit).
3. Total up the two columns. If they balance, the job is done! If not, proceed as follows.
4. Look for an error of complete omission of an account balance in the trial balance, or of one side of a posting in the ledger. You should spot this if you look for a figure equal to the error.
5. If this fails, look for an error due to something being entered on the wrong side of the trial balance, or to both sides of a transaction being posted to the same side in the ledger. Divide the discrepancy in your trial balance by two, and look for a figure which matches this.
6. If this fails, look for an error of transposition. Is the discrepancy divisible by nine? If so, there could well be such an error. If these methods all fail, the error could be in the totalling up, or in under- or overstating one side of a transaction, or a mixture of errors.
7. Check through the ledger again to look for any folio column omissions.
8. Check off each ledger balance against the trial balance. Have you recorded it on the correct side? Tick each in pencil as you go. If this does not solve the problem, proceed to step 9.
9. Re-check the addition of all your ledger columns, and balance each account. If this still doesn't solve the problem proceed to step 10.
10. Check that the values in the posting of both sides of each transaction are equal. Start at the first page of the ledger and work through to the end. Tick each in pencil as you go.

TRIAL BALANCE

trading, profit & loss account items   balance sheet items

	Dr.	Cr.		Dr.	Cr.
Purchases	28,879.00		Cash	50.00	
Sales		48,133.00	Bank	981.00	
Heat & Light	400.00		Land & Bldgs	490,000.00	
Motor Expenses	1,480.00		Machinery	100,000.00	
Insurance	240.00		Fixtures &		
			Fittings	60,000.00	
Wages	6,913.00		Motor vehicles	80,000.00	
Salaries	3,000.00		Debtors	2,010.00	
Stock	3,600.00		Creditors		3,190.00
			Capital		178,199.00
			Long-term		
			creditor		548,031.00
	44,512.00	48,133.00		733,041.00	729,420.00
				44,512.00	48,133.00
				777,553.00	777,553.00

Fig. 48. Example of a four column trial balance using the
same figures as on page 70.

If you have carried out all the steps accurately, the trial balance will
now balance. Note: a small error need not hold up the preparation of
final accounts; you can post the error to a 'Suspense Account' to save
time. When eventually the error is tracked down a 'Statement of
amended profit or loss' can be drawn up.

The four column trial balance

A variation of the trial balance described above is the four column
version. This is simply one with two debit columns and two credit
columns. In fact the page is most usefully split down the middle so
that each side can have its own debit and credit columns. On one side
you enter all the balances relating to the revenue accounts. On the
other side you enter those which relate to the balance sheet. On each
side you total up the debit and credit columns separately to give either
a debit or credit balance. If things are right the debit balance on one
side will equal the credit balance on the other.

28 The trial balance: errors

Errors revealed and errors not revealed

The trial balance will immediately show that there is an error if it does not balance. However, it will not guarantee that the posting is error free if it does. In other words, things cannot be right if it does not balance, but can still be wrong if it does! Furthermore, a failure to balance does not tell us where in the posting the error or errors exist. So while the trial balance performs something of an error-checking role, it is not a foolproof one.

Errors not revealed

1. Errors of complete omission, where neither debit nor credit has been entered.

2. Compensating errors, where errors of equal value cancel each other out.

3. Errors of commision—posting to the wrong accounts, though to the correct sides of the correct ledger division.

4. Errors of reverse posting: the debit entry of a transaction has been wrongly posted to the credit side, and vice versa. (See also page 148.)

5. Errors of principle, for example posting of an asset to an expenses account.

Errors which will be revealed by a trial balance

1. Errors arising from both parts of the double entry (debit/credit) being posted to the same side (e.g. debit).

2. Errors of partial omission, for example, where only one side of a transaction was posted, such as the credit side but not the debit side, or vice versa.

3. Errors in adding up.

4. Errors of transposition, where digits have been accidentally reversed, for example 54 has been written as 45. See page 149 for how to identify this error.

5. Errors due to under- or overstating one side of the transaction.

6. Errors of original entry, for example when making a mistake while entering a sales invoice into the sales day book.

				Electricity			
200X					200X		
Mar	1	Balance	b/d	2,100	Mar 31	Profit and Loss	2,520
	31	Balance	c/d	420			
				2,520			2,520
					Apr 1	Balance b/d	420

Fig. 49. Example of an accrual for electricity charges.

				Insurance			
200X					200X		
Mar	31	Balance	b/d	230	Mar 31	Profit and Loss	120
					31	Balance c/d	110
				230			230
Apr	1	Balance	b/d	110			

Fig. 50. Example of prepayment of insurance.

1. Suppose A. Frazer's insurance premium of £1,200 is payable yearly in advance from 1 June, but its accounting year runs from 1 May. By the end of the accounting year only 11 months of the premium will have been used up, there will still be an asset of 1 month's prepaid premium to carry forward to the next year. This is how it will appear in the ledger:

				Insurance			
200X					200X		
June	1	Bank		1,200	Apr 31	Profit & Loss	1,100
						Prepayment c/d	100
				1,200			1,200
Prepayment			b/d	100			

Fig. 51. Worked example of the posting of a prepayment.

2. Suppose that aggregate weekly wages of £1,500 are payable on a Friday and the end of the firm's acounting year falls on a Tuesday. There will be a liability for 3 days aggregated, unpaid wages to account for in the end of year accounts. This is how it will appear:

				Wages A/C			
200X					200X		
Aug	31	Balance	b/d	77,100	Aug 31	Profit and Loss A/C	78,000
	31	Accruals	c/d	900			
				78,000			78,000
					Sep 1	Accruals b/d	900

Fig. 52. Worked example of the posting of an accrual.

29 Accruals and prepayments

Adjustments to accounts

Accruals and prepayments are adjustments we need to make to the accounts at the end of the year (or other management accounting period).

- Accruals are sometimes called accrued expenses, expense creditors or expenses owing. Accruals are a liability for expenses for goods or services already consumed, but not yet billed (invoiced).

- Prepayments are an asset of goods or services already paid for, but not yet completely used. Prepayments are, therefore, in a sense the opposite of accruals.

Example of accrued expenses

Suppose we are drawing up accounts for the year ended 31st March. We know there will be an electricity bill for the three months ended 30th April, a month after the end of our financial year. By 31st March, even though we haven't had the bill, we would already have used two months' worth of it, but as things stand the cost of this won't appear in our accounts because it is too soon to have received a source document (i.e. the invoice) from which to enter it. Still, electricity clearly was an expense during the period, so we have to 'accrue' a sensible proportion. For example:

Electricity account period	1st February to 30th April
Estimated charge	£630.00 (three month period)
Period falling within our accounts	1st February to 31st March (two months)

Charged accrued for period: $£630.00 \times \dfrac{2 \text{ months}}{3 \text{ months}} = £420.00$

Wages and rent

Other items that often have to be accrued are wages and rent. The firm receives the benefit of work, and of premises, before it pays out wages and rent (assuming rents are payable in arrears; if rent is payable in advance we would need to treat it as a prepayment).

ACCRUALS	PREPAYMENTS
The balance c/d will be a debit one, but the ultimate effect on the expense account (the balance b/d) will be a credit entry.	The balance c/d will be a credit one, but the ultimate effect on the expense account (the balance b/d) will be a debit entry.

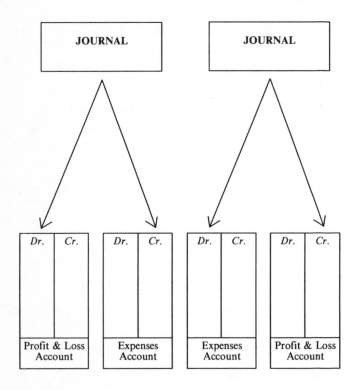

Fig. 53. Accruals and prepayments at a glance.

29 Accruals and prepayments—cont.

Example of prepayment

A prepayment arises, for example, where an insurance premium or professional subscription is paid annually in advance but only one or two month's benefit has been used by the end of the year. We must adjust the figures so that we don't charge the whole amount against profits for the year. Clearly, much of the benefit remains as an asset for use in the next year. Example, again assuming that our accounting period ends on 31st March:

Professional subscription for calendar year:	£100.00
Period falling within our accounts:	1st January to 31st March
Period falling into next accounting period	1st April to 31st December (9 months)
Prepaid for next year:	$£100.00 \times \dfrac{9}{12} = £75.00$

Carrying down accruals and prepayments

When these amounts have been calculated or assessed, you place them in the relevant ledger accounts as 'carried down' balances. In this way you increase or decrease the amount to be transferred to the Profit and Loss Account for the year, depending on which side the posting is made. The resulting 'b/d' balances are listed in the balance sheet just like any other balance remaining on the nominal ledger at the end of the year. If they are credit balances (accruals) they are current liabilities. If they are debit balances (prepayments) they are assets.

THE TRADING ACCOUNT

1 Sales

2 Purchases

3 Opening stock

4 Closing stock

5 Carriage Inwards (and any Warehousing and Packaging costs)

Fig. 54. Items listed in a Trading Account. Remember the mnemonic SPOCC.

TYPICAL PROFIT & LOSS ACCOUNT ITEMS

Wages and Salaries

Heat and Light

Rent and Rates

Motor Expenses

Bank Charges

Bad Debts

Depreciation

Insurance

Carriage Outwards

There can be many more; it just depends on the type of business.

Fig. 55. Items listed in a Profit & Loss Account.

30 Revenue accounts

The trading account and profit & loss account
The revenue accounts are a pair of ledger accounts called the trading account and the profit & loss account. They are much like any other ledger account except that they are not ongoing (except for limited companies, dealt with later). Also, they are needed by more people outside the firm for example:

- the Inland Revenue to assess tax liability
- shareholders to see how the business is doing
- prospective purchasers to value the business
- prospective lenders to assess the risk of lending to the business, and its ability to pay interest.

But we adapt these accounts to a more easy-to-read version. Instead of two main columns we have only one (though we also use subsidiary columns for calculations). The two sides of the accounts are then represented in progressive stages of addition and subtraction. So the revenue accounts forwarded to interested parties don't look like ledger accounts at all.

The trading account
This shows the gross profit, and how it is worked out:
 sales − cost of goods sold = gross profit
To work out the cost of goods sold (i.e. cost of sales):

 purchases + opening stock + carriage inwards, packaging and warehouse costs − closing stock = cost of sales

When transferring the balances to the trading acount, deduct sales returns from sales, before posting in the trading account. After all, they are merely 'un-sales' so to speak. The same goes for purchase returns: there is no place for any returns in the trading account.

The profit & loss account
The profit & loss account sets out the calculation of net profit like this:

 gross profit + other income − expenses = net profit

We know that there must be two sides to every ledger posting: as you post each item in the revenue accounts, make an opposite side posting in the original ledger account from where your balance came. Against such postings just write 'trading account' or 'profit & loss' account. You are now closing down the revenue and expense ledger accounts, ready for a fresh start in the next accounting period.

Trading Account			
Sales			100,000
Purchases		58,000	
Opening stock	12,000		
Closing stock	10,000	2,000	60,000
Gross Profit			40,000

Balance Sheet (extract from)		
Current Assets		
Stock	10,000	
Debtors	8,000	
Cash at Bank	2,000	
Cash in hand	50	20,050

Fig. 56. Stock appears three times in the final accounts. Closing stock appears twice (although it is conventional to only use the adjective 'Closing' in the Trading Account to distinguish it from 'Opening stock').

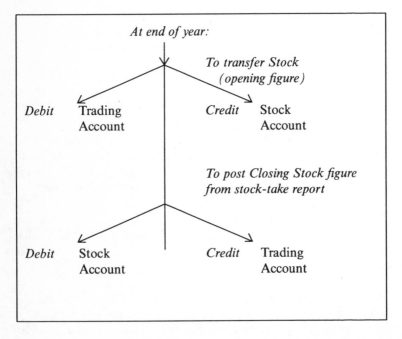

Fig. 57. What to do about stock at the end of the year.

31 Stock in the final accounts

Opening and closing stock

Stock is dealt with three times in the revenue accounts and balance sheet—once as opening stock and twice as closing stock. Suppose we started the year with £1,000 worth of stock; we purchased a further £10,000 of stock during the year, but had none left at the end of it. Altogether, it means that we have sold assets of £11,000 during the year. Purchases and opening stock must be the same kind of asset, since they were both finished goods on the shelf; otherwise we could not have sold them both and had nothing left to sell. Clearly, stock and purchases need to be treated in the same way in the final accounts.

This year's opening stock was, in fact, last year's closing stock. Throughout this year it was an asset, appearing on the debit side of the ledger. So this year's closing stock must also be carried forward to the next year as an asset; it too must stay on the ledger, just like all other assets at the end of the year. The only balances we must transfer out permanently to the revenue accounts are those for expenses and revenues (which of course are not assets).

Physical stock-take

Closing stock will not even be in the ledger until we have done a stock-take (a physical counting and valuation of the stock in hand). We must then post to the debit side of the stock account in the nominal ledger the actual asset value of stock remaining, and being carried forward into next year.

Why we need a counter-entry for stock

The counter-entry must be posted to the credit of the trading account. Why? Let us go back to our basic example. We posted opening stock as a debit in the trading account because we assumed it had all been sold, along with the purchases for that year. But what if we bought £12,000 worth but still had £2,000 worth left? We will need to make an entry to the opposite side for this. Closing stock is a credit posting in the trading account.

Another way to look at it is this: if we purchased £12,000 worth of stock but only sold £10,000, it would be as if we had purchased only £10,000 worth for sale during the year. The other £2,000 worth would be for sale in the next year. So we are right to deduct closing stock from purchases.

Remember, a credit posting in the final accounts can also be done as a subtraction from the debit column. You have to do this when converting the ledger format to vertical format (see page 84).

```
                Trading Account for A. Frazer
                for Year Ended 31 March 200X
                       £           £          £
Sales                                       90,000
Less Cost of Sales:
  Purchases                      50,000
  Opening stock      6,000
    Less Closing Stock 2,000      4,000     54,000
Gross Profit                                36,000
```

Fig. 58. Worked example of revenue accounts.

1. From the following ledger balances draw up the Trading Account of A. Frazer for the year ended 31 March 200X.

Sales £90,000
Purchases £50,000
Stock (from ledger) £6,000
Stock (from final stock-take) £2,000

2. From the following ledger balances draw up the Revenue Accounts of A. T. Office Supplies for year ended 30 April 200X.

Sales	180,000
Purchases	100,000
Ledger balance for Stock	6,000
Stock as per final stock-take	14,000
Heat and Light	1,000
Motor Expenses	1,500
Bank Charges	500
Rent	3,000
Wages	37,000
Insurance	2,000

```
        Trading, Profit & Loss Account for A. T. Office Supplies
                  for the Year Ended 30 April 200X
                       £           £          £
Sales                                      180,000
Less Cost of Sales:
  Purchases                     100,000
  Opening stock      6,000
    Less Closing Stock 14,000    (8,000)    92,000
Gross Profit                                88,000

Wages                            37,000
Heat and Light                    1,000
Rent                              3,000
Motor Expenses                    1,500
Bank charges                        500
Insurance                         2,000     45,000
Net Profit                                  43,000
```

Fig. 59. Further worked example of revenue accounts.

32   How to compile revenue accounts

What you will need
- the trial balance
- the ledger (all divisions)
- details of end of year adjustments to the accounts, such as depreciation, bad debts, closing stock
- the journal.

Adjustments before you start
You will need to adjust the trial balance for various end of year adjustments. Remember to enter all your adjustments into the trial balance twice, once on the debit side and once on the credit side. You can achieve the same effect by adding to and subtracting from the same side as, indeed, you would need to with accruals and prepayments. For a prepayment for example, you would debit 'prepayments' in the trial balance, and subtract the same amount from the debit balance of the expense account concerned, e.g. 'Insurance'. Check that the trial balance still balances after you have adjusted it: there is no point in starting to put together your final accounts until it is correct.

Getting the right balance into the right accounts
It is a good idea to label each balance, to show where it will go in your final accounts. For example against 'sales' write 'T' 'for trading acccount'. Write 'P & L' beside 'rent & rates' to show that it is going into the profit and loss account. Write 'B' beside each asset account, to show you will be taking it into your balance sheet.

Items on the debit side of the trial balance are expenses or assets; those on the credit side are revenues or liabilities. In the revenue accounts we are only interested in revenues and expenses. How do we recognise them?

A revenue is an income; an expense is an outgoing. Neither has to be in cash. If you have more stock left at the end than you had at the beginning of the accounting period, that is just as much a revenue as a sales figure. Another way of putting it is to say that excesses of expenses over revenues are called losses. Expenses represent an outflow of funds within the period. They include such things as electricity, motor expenses, rents paid or payable, and discounts allowed. Items classed as revenues represent incomes within the same period. They include things like commissions, rents receivable, and discounts received.

A. FRAZER
Trading Profit and Loss Account
for Year Ended 31 March 200X

Stock as at 1 April 200X	10,000	Sales	100,000
Purchases	60,000	Stock as at	
Carriage Inwards	3,000	31 March 200X	9,000
Gross Profit c/d	36,000		
	109,000		109,000
		Gross Profit b/d	36,000

Profit and Loss Account

Wages	6,000		
Motor Expenses	2,000		
Heat and Light	450		
Cleaning	1,500		
Depreciation	2,550		
Net Profit c/d	23,500		
	36,000		36,000
		Net Profit b/d to	
		Capital Account	23,500

Fig. 60. Trading Profit and Loss Account in horizontal format in the Ledger. This can now easily be transformed into the more useful vertical format shown below.

A. FRAZER
Trading Profit and Loss Account
for Year Ended 31 March 200X

Sales			100,000
Less Purchases		60,000	
Carriage inwards		3,000	
Opening stock	10,000		
Less closing stock	9,000	1,000	64,000
Gross Profit b/d			36,000
Less Expenses			
Wages	6,000		
Motor Expenses	2,000		
Heat and Light	450		
Cleaning	1,500		
Depreciation	2,550		12,500
Net Profit b/d to Capital Account			23,500

Fig. 61. Trading Profit & Loss Account in vertical format.

33   Compiling revenue accounts step-by-step

Once you have labelled each item in the trial balance according to where it will go in the final accounts you can put together your revenue accounts as follows.

1. Write in the next available space in the 'Particulars' column of the journal: 'Sales'.
2. In the debit column, enter the balance of your sales account.
3. Beneath the last entry in the 'Particulars' column, write: 'trading account' (indenting it slightly).
4. Enter the same figure in the credit cash column.
5. In the next space in the 'Particulars' column, write: 'trading account'.
6. Enter in the debit/cash column the balance of your purchases account.
7. Write in the next space in the 'Particulars' column (indenting slightly) the name of the account from which you are transferring (in this case 'Purchases') and enter the value of purchases in the credit cash columns.
8. Repeat steps 5 to 8 for each of the other categories in the 'cost of sales' equation (see page 79).
9. When you have made all the entries relating to the trading account, write beneath them: 'To close revenue and expense accounts and transfer the balances to the trading account'.
10. Now do the same for any other income accounts (items other than 'trading income', e.g. rents). Debit the accounts concerned. Credit your profit & loss account.
11. Now do the same for each of the overhead expense accounts. Debit your profit & loss account and credit each account concerned.
12. When you have made all the entries for your profit and loss account, write underneath: 'To close expense accounts and transfer balances to profit & loss account.'
13. Now post to the ledger, including a trading, profit & loss account, exactly following the instructions you have just written in your journal (see page 48 for ledger posting). The trading, profit & loss account can be seen as two divisions of the same account, since they are written on the same page. The balance of the fomer is brought down to the latter, and marked: 'Gross profit b/d' (see opposite page, top).
14. Total up and balance all the ledger accounts concerned. This will mean closing all but the trading profit & loss account (except where an accrual or prepayment is present).
15. Mark the balance of profit & loss account: 'Net profit c/d to capital account'.

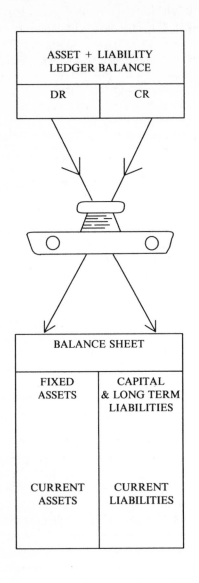

Fig. 62. The balance sheet as a snapshot of the financial affairs.

34 The balance sheet

A financial snapshot

We have already seen standard sorts of statement summarising particular aspects of the business. The bank reconciliation was an example. The balance sheet is another—but a much more important one. Unlike the trading, profit and loss account, the balance sheet is not an 'account' as such. Rather, it is a useful snapshot of the firm's financial situation at a fixed point in time. It sets out clearly all the firm's assets and liabilities, and shows how the resulting net assets are matched by the capital account.

The balance sheet always goes hand-in-hand with the trading, profit and loss account. We need it to show:

- where the net profit has gone (or how the net loss has been paid for)
- how any net profit has been added to the capital account
- how much has been taken out as 'drawings' and whether any of it has been used to buy new assets (stating what those assets are).

Management data

Accounting ratios can be worked out to help decision-making. For example the ratio of current assets/current liabilities shows how easily a firm can pay its debts as they become due (a ratio of 2/1 is often seen as acceptable in this respect). More will be said about these ratios later.

Five main components of the balance sheet

The balance sheet tells us about five main categories:

1. Fixed assets. These are assets the business intends to keep for a long time (at least for the year in question). They include things like premises, fixtures and fittings, machinery and motor vehicles. Fixed assets are not for using up in day to day production or trading (though a small part of their value is used up in wear and tear, and that is treated as an expense—'depreciation').

2. Current assets. These are assets used up in day to day trading or production. They include such things as stock, debtors, cash at bank and cash in hand.

3. Current liabilities. These are amounts the business owes to creditors, and which usually have to be paid within the next accounting year. They include trade creditors, and bank overdraft.

A. FRAZER
BALANCE SHEET
As at 31 December 200X

	Cost	Less Provision for Depreciation	Net Book Value
Fixed assets			
Premises	40,000		40,000
Fixtures and fittings	15,000	750	14,250
Motor Van	8,000	1,600	6,400
	63,000	2,350	60,650
Current assets			
Stock		9,000	
Debtors	10,000		
Less Provision for doubtful debts	2,000	8,000	
Cash at Bank		10,000	
Cash in Hand		50	
		27,050	
Current liabilities			
Creditors		12,000	
Total Net Assets (or working capital)			15,050
			75,700
Financed by			
Capital as at 1 January 200X			63,150
Add profit for period			19,100
			82,250
Less drawings			6,550
			75,700

Fig. 63. Example of a balance sheet in vertical format.

A. FRAZER
BALANCE SHEET
As at 31 December 200X

Fixed Assets			Capital	
Premises		40,000	Balance as at 1 January 200X	63,150
Fixture and fittings	15,000		Add profit for year	19,100
Less provision for depreciation	750	14,250		82,250
			Less Drawings	6,550
				75,700
Motor van	8,000			
Less provision for depreciation	1,600	6,400		
		60,650		
Current Assets				
Stock		9,000	Current Liabilities	12,000
Debtors	10,000			
Less provision for bad debts	2,000	8,000		
Cash at Bank		10,000		
Cash in Hand		50		
		87,700		87,700

Fig. 64. Example of a balance sheet in horizontal format.

35 Compiling a balance sheet step-by-step

4. Long-term liabilities. A business may also have financial obligations which do not have to be settled within the next accounting year. These include such things as long term loans, for example to buy plant, equipment, vehicles or property.

5. Capital. This means the property of the owner of the business. He has invested his personal property in the business—cash, any other assets, and profits ploughed back. The business holds the value of all this for him in safe-keeping; it must deliver it up to him on cessation of the business, or earlier if he requires. Capital is, in a way, a liability to the business; but it's a rather different one from the other liabilities, which is why we don't include it with them.

Postings to capital account
There are four types of posting we may need to make to capital account in the ledger: opening capital, extra capital injections, drawings, and the addition of profit.

Terminology
'Capital' should not be confused with 'working capital', which is a very different thing (current assets—current liabilities). And do not confuse capital with capital expenditure, which just means expenditure on fixed assets rather than on expenses.

If the books have been written up correctly, the assets and liabilities must balance against capital in the balance sheet, to embody the equation we first saw on page 13:

$$\text{assets} - \text{liabilities} = \text{capital}$$

What you need

- the trial balance 'adjusted' or 'redrafted' after compilation of the trading, profit & loss account to show the stock figure and the profit or loss.

Preparation
Make sure that the balances listed on the trial balance that have already been used in the trading, profit & loss account are clearly ticked off. The remaining balances can then easily be spotted for use in compiling the balance sheet.

BALANCE SHEET OF A. FRAZER
as at 30 June 200X

Fixed Assets			
Land and Buildings			200,000
Fixtures and fittings		50,000	
Less provision for depreciation		12,000	38,000
Office Machinery		100,000	
Less provisions for depreciation		15,000	85,000
Motor Van		50,000	
Less provision for depreciation		30,000	20,000
			343,000
CURRENT ASSETS			
Stock		40,000	
Debtors	33,000		
Less provision for bad debts	1,000	32,000	
Cash at Bank		3,950	
Cash in Hand		50	
		76,000	
Less CURRENT LIABILITIES			
Creditors		35,000	
Working Capital			41,000
			384,000
Represented by			
Opening Capital			347,777
Less Drawings			9,950
			337,827
Add Profit			46,173
Closing Capital			384,000

Fig. 65. Balance sheet of A. Frazer in vertical format.

From the following details construct a Balance Sheet as at 30 June 200X in vertical format for A. Frazer (answer above).

Land and buildings	200,000
Office Machinery	100,000
Motor Van	50,000
Fixture and fittings	50,000
Provision for depreciation on Machinery	15,000
Provision for depreciation on motor van	30,000
Provision for depreciation on fixtures and fittings	12,000
Closing stock	40,000
Cash at Bank	3,950
Cash in Hand	50
Drawings	9,950
Debtors	33,000
Creditors	35,000
Bad debts provision	1,000
Capital	347,777
Net Profit	46,173

35   Compiling the balance sheet—cont.

1. Make a heading 'Balance Sheet of [firm] as at [date].
2. Make a sub-heading on the left, 'Fixed Assets'.
3. Beneath this, in column three, write the value of any premises. Annotate it; on the left 'Land and Buildings'.
4. In column two, list the balance of other fixed assets, in order of permanence. Annotate each one on the far left. Beneath each one record the provision for depreciation, annotating 'Less provision for depreciation'.
5. Subtract the depreciation from each asset and place the difference in column three.
6. Total up column three.
7. Now make a second sub-heading, 'Current Assets'.
8. Beneath this, in the second cash column, write the balances of the short-life assets, in the order of permanence, annotating accordingly.
9. Total up these balances.
10. Make a third sub-heading on the left, 'Less Current Liabilities'.
11. Below that, list, in the first cash column, the creditors figure and the bank overdraft figure, if there is one.
12. Total up this column. Place the total in the second column beneath that for current assets. If there is only one item you can place it directly into the second column.
13. Now rule off this column and subtract the latter total from the former. Place the difference in the third column below the total for fixed assets, annotating it 'Working Capital'. Add these two totals and rule off with a double line, annotating it 'Total Net Assets'.
14. Make a sub-heading below this, 'Represented by'.
15. Enter the opening capital in the third column, annotating it 'Opening Capital'.
16. Enter the drawings balance, annotating it 'Less Drawings'.
17. Rule off and deduct.
18. Enter the profit in column three, annotating it 'Add Profit'.
19. Rule off and add. Underline the answer with double line and annotate it 'Closing Capital'.

Horizontal and vertical formats
A balance sheet may be shown in horizontal or vertical format. Unless told otherwise, use the vertical format in exams and in practice.

ARMSTRONG ENGINEERING
Manufacturing Account
as at 31 December 200X

Raw Materials

Opening Stock		10,000
Add Purchases		102,000
		112,000
Less Closing Stock		12,000
Cost of Raw Materials Consumed		100,000
Manufacturing Wages		200,000
Prime Cost		300,000

Overhead costs

Rent (½)	10,000	
Rates (½)	2,000	
Heat, Light and Power ($^3/_4$)	8,000	20,000
		320,000

Adjustment for Work in Progress

Opening Stock	12,000	
Less Closing Stock	15,000	(3,000)
Cost of Finished Goods		
Transferred to Trading Account		317,000

Fig. 66. Simple example of a manufacturing account.

Part of the revenue accounts

Like the trading account, the manufacturing account is part of the revenue accounts. Its format is similar, but it has quite different components. It is used when we want to show the manufacturing costs involved in the production of goods. This final cost of production is transferred from the manufacturing account to the trading account. For a manufacturing firm this figure is the equivalent of purchases for a purely trading firm.

36   Manufacturing accounts

We need to show two important cost figures in the manufacturing account:

- **prime cost**—the sum of the costs of direct labour, direct materials and direct expenses; and

- **overheads**—the sum of all costs which cannot be directly related to output (e.g. factory rent).

Three stages of the production process are shown in a manufacturing account:

1.   Raw materials consumed.

2.   Adjustment for stocks of partly finished goods (work in progress).

3.   Finished goods transferred to trading account.

The cost of raw material consumed is arrived at like this:

Opening stocks	600
Add Purchases	200
	800
Less Closing stocks	150
Cost of raw material consumed	650

The prime cost is found by adding the direct wages and direct expenses to cost of raw materials consumed.
  Work in progress is calculated similarly:

Opening stocks	600
Less Closing stocks	150
Work in progress adj.	450

Purchases do not come into this equation.
  The end product of the manufacturing account is the value of the stock of finished goods (just as the gross profit is the end product of the trading account). This value is then transferred to the trading account, just as the trading account transfers its gross profit to the profit & loss account.

Manufacturing Account of Armstrong Engineering
for the year ended 31 October 200X

Stock of raw materials as at 1.11.200X		4,000
Add Purchases		40,000
		44,000
Less Stock of raw materials as at 31.10.200X		5,500
Cost of raw materials consumed		38,500
Add Direct labour		4,500
Prime cost		43,000
Factory overheads		1,600
		44,600
Add Work in progress as at 1.11.200X	8,000	
Less Work in progress as at 31.10.200X	9,500	(1,500)
Cost of finished goods transferred		
to Trading Account		43,100

Fig. 67. Worked example of a manufacturing account.

Suppose Armstrong Engineering is a manufacturer who at the end of the year to 31 October 200X has a stock of raw materials valued at £5,500 and work in progress valued at £9,500. The firm started the year with a stock of raw materials worth £4,000 and work in progress valued at £8,000. During the year it purchased a further £40,000's worth. The factory wages bill was £4,500 and the cost of power used solely in the factory was £1,600.

Figure 67 shows how you would write up its manufacturing account.

37   Compiling a manufacturing account step-by-step

1. Calculate the cost of raw materials consumed. Write the correct heading against each line of your calculation.

2. Add the figures for direct wages and direct expenses, annotating accordingly.

3. Annotate the total 'prime cost'.

4. In a subsidiary column, itemise the various overhead expenses. Note: it may be that only part (e.g. half) of a cost (e.g. rent) can be fairly attributed to the manufacturing process, the other part being more fairly attributed for example to Sales. In such a case, only the first part should be itemised. Just mark it like this: 'Rent (½)'.

5. Total up this column. Place the total in the main cash column and total that column.

6. In the subsidiary column write your work in progress adjustment (see formula on page 93). Write the correct heading against each line of your calculation. Place the resultant figure in your main cash column and add or deduct it from your subtotal according to whether it is a positive or negative figure.

7. Write against the difference: 'Cost of finished goods transferred to trading account'.

	£	£
Cost		100,000
Less Estimated residual value		3,000
Amount to be depreciated over 5 years		
Provision for Depreciation		
Yr 1 97,000 × 0.2 =	19,400	
Yr 2 97,000 × 0.2 =	19,400	
Yr 3 97,000 × 0.2 =	19,400	
Yr 4 97,000 × 0.2 =	19,400	
Yr 5 97,000 × 0.2 =	19,400	
	97,000	97,000

Fig. 68. Worked example of depreciation using the straight line method.

1. Suppose a lorry costing £100,000 had an estimated lifespan within the company of 5 years and an estimated residual value at the end of that period of £3,000.

Using the straight line method and a rate of 20% the effect would be as shown in Figure 68.

38 Depreciation: the straight line method

When assets drop in value

So far we have recorded figures, analysed them, summed and balanced them, and learned the standard ways of doing so. Now, with depreciation, we will also need to make calculations involving percentages.

Depreciation is the drop in value of an asset due to age, wear and tear. This drop in value is a drain on the firm's resources, and so we must put it in the accounts as an expense. We will need to write down the value of the asset in the books, to reflect its value more realistically. A company car, for example, loses value over time. So do plant, equipment and other assets. All have to be written down each year.

Methods of calculating depreciation

- straight line method
- diminishing (or reducing) balance method
- sum of the digits method
- machine hours method
- revaluation method
- depletion method
- sinking fund method
- sinking fund with endowment method.

Even this list is not exhaustive. But the first two are the most common.

The straight line method

This involves deducting a fixed percentage of the asset's initial book value, minus the estimated residual value, each year. The estimated residual value means the value at the end of its useful life within the business (which may be scrap value). The percentage deducted each year is usually 20% or $33^1/_3$% and reflects the estimated annual fall in the asset's value. Suppose the firm buys a motor van for £12,100; it expects it to get very heavy use during the first three years, after which it would only be worth £100 for scrap. Each year we would write it down by one third of its initial value minus the estimated residual value, i.e. £4,000 per year. On the other hand, suppose we buy a company car for £12,300; we expect it to get only average use and to be regularly serviced. We expect to sell it after five years for £4,800. In that case we would write down the difference of £7,500 by one fifth (20%) each year, i.e. £1,500 per year.

		£	£
Cost			100,000
Depreciation Provision Year	1	50,000	
	2	25,000	
	3	12,500	
	4	6,250	
	5	3,125	96,875
Residual value after 5 years			3,125

2. Suppose a machine cost £100,000 and it is estimated that at the end of 5 years it will be sold for £3,125. Suppose also that the greatest usage of the machine will be in the early years as will also the greatest costs, for since it is tailor-made for the firm's requirements its resale value is drastically reduced the moment it is installed. The appropriate rate of depreciation on the diminishing balance method will be between 2 and 3 times that for the straight line method, so an acceptable rate will be 50%.

39 Depreciation: the diminishing balance method

This method also applies a fixed percentage, but it applies it to the diminishing value of the asset each year—not to the initial value. It is used for assets which have a long life within the firm, and where the biggest drop in value comes in the early years, getting less as time goes on.

Suppose a lathe in an engineering workshop cost £40,000 to buy. In the first year it will fall in value much more than it ever will in later years. The guarantee may expire at the end of the first year. The bright smooth paint on the surface will be scratched and scarred; the difference between its appearance when new and its appearance a year later will be quite obvious. But the next year the change will seem less; who will notice a few more scratches on an already scarred surface? Nor will there be a great drop due to the guarantee expiring, for it will not have started out with one at the beginning of the second year. And so it will go on; the value of the asset will depreciate by smaller and smaller amounts throughout its life. Most people would agree that a three-year-old machine has less value than an otherwise identical two-year-old one, but who could say that a 16-year-old machine really has any less value than a 15-year-old one? Since the value of these assets erodes in smaller and smaller amounts as the years go by, we use the diminishing balance method of calculation.

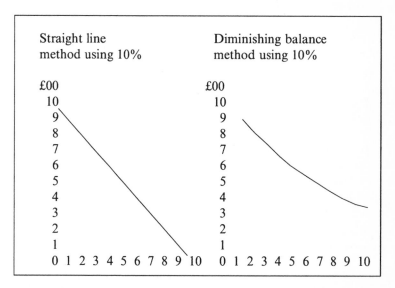

Fig. 69. Common methods of depreciation. The figure of 10% is used in both cases to illustrate the comparison (it is not necessarily the most common percentage to be used).

40 Other methods of depreciation

The sum of the digits method

This method is more common in the USA than in Britain. It works in the opposite way to the diminishing balance method. The latter applies a constant percentage but to a progressively reducing balance, but the sum of the digits method applies a progressively small percentage to a constant figure (the initial cost figure). It is called the sum of the digits method because it involves summing the individual year numbers in the expected life span of the asset to arrive at the denominator of a fraction to be applied in calculating depreciation each year. The numerator is the year number concerned, in a reverse order.

For example if an asset had an expected useful life of 5 years then in year 1 the numerator would be 5, and in year 2 it would be 4 and so on, until year 5 when the numerator would be 1. Supposing an asset was expected to last 10 years before becoming worthless: we would add $1 + 2 + 3 + 4 + 5 + 6 + 7 + 8 + 9 + 10 = 55$. In year one, we would depreciate by multiplying the original value by 10/55, in year 2 by 9/55 and so on until year 10 when we would write it down by only 1/55 of its initial value.

The machine hours method

We divide the initial cost value of a machine by the estimated number of machine hours in its useful life. The depreciation charge is then calculated by multiplying this quotient by the number of hours the machine has been used within the accounting year.

The revaluation method

This method means revaluing the asset each year. It may involve observation, and item counting, and taking into account factors such as current market prices.

It is useful in respect of small tools, for example, for which it would be silly to keep a separate asset account and provision for depreciation account for each little item. Revaluing is also useful in dealing with livestock, for their values go up and down; a dairy cow for example will be less valuable when very young than when fully grown, but then its value will decline as it gets old. Throughout its life this rise and fall in value may be further affected by changes in food prices in the market place. If revaluation is used, no provision for depreciation is needed.

40   Other methods of depreciation—cont.

The depletion method
This is used in the adjusting of values of ore bodies, mines, quarries and oil wells. The initial value of the mine etc is divided by the quantity of ore or mineral that it contained at the beginning; the quotient is then multiplied by the quantity *actually* mined in the accounting year to give the amount of depletion in value.

The sinking fund method
This method, as well as depreciating an asset's value in the books, builds up a fund for replacing it at the end of its useful life. A compound interest formula is applied to the estimated cost of replacement at the end of the asset's life; it shows how much money must be invested each year (outside the firm) to provide the replacement fund when the time comes. This amount is then charged annually to the Profit and Loss Account as Depreciation. The credit entry is posted to a Depreciation Fund Account. The amount is then suitably invested and the asset which thereby comes into existence is debited to a depreciation fund investment account, the credit entry obviously going to bank. This method is not popular now because there is so much uncertainty about inflation and interest rates.

The sinking fund with endowment policy method
This is similar but uses an endowment policy to generate the replacement fund on maturity. The premium is payable annually in advance.

JOURNAL

200X Particulars		Fo.	Debit	Credit
June 30	Profit and Loss	NL30	50,000	
	Provision for			
	Depreciation on			
	machines	NL8		50,000
	Profit and Loss	NL30	19,400	
	Provision for			
	Depreciation			
	on lorry	NL9		19,400

LEDGER

NL8   *Provision for depreciation on machine*

Dr.				Cr.
200X		200X		
		June 30	Profit & Loss	50,000

NL9   *Provision for depreciation on motor lorry*

Dr.				Cr.
200X		200X		
		June 30	Profit & Loss	19,400

NL30   *Profit and Loss Account*

Dr.			Cr.
200X		200X	
June 30	Depreciation	69,400	

Fig. 70. Worked example of depreciation accounting. This is how the depreciation in the worked examples on pages 96-98 would be written at the end of the year. The same would be the case for the subsequent years, except, of course, that the values would be different in respect of the machine depreciation.

41 Depreciation step-by-step

What you need

- the nominal ledger

- scrap paper for your calculations

- the journal.

Step-by-step

1. Decide what kind of asset is concerned, what pattern of erosion applies to it and so which method of depreciation is best.

2. Calculate the annual depreciation figure for the asset.

3. In the next available space in the journal, write the date in the date column, and 'Profit & loss' in the 'Particulars' column. Remember, never post directly to the ledger—only via a book of prime entry (in this case the journal, a useful book for miscellaneous recordings like depreciation).

4. Enter the amount of depreciation in the debit cash column.

5. Underneath the last entry in the 'Particulars' column, indenting slightly, write: 'Provision for depreciation on [name of asset]'.

6. Enter the same value in the credit cash column.

7. Repeat for any other assets you need to depreciate in the accounts.

8. Open a 'Provision for Depreciation' account for each asset concerned. Record the page numbers in the index.

9. Make postings to each of these ledger accounts, following the instructions you have just written in the journal.

Note

A Statement of Standard Accounting Practice (SSAP) was issued in December 1977 and revised in 1981 for the treatment of depreciation in accounts (SSAP12). The student can refer to this for further information if desired.

SALES LEDGER

p2   p2

H. Baker

Date 200X	Particulars	Fo.	Totals	Date 200X	Particulars	Fo.	Totals
Jun 30	Sales	NL6	200.00	Mar 31	Bad Debts	NL20	200.00

NOMINAL LEDGER

p20   p20

Bad Debts Account

Date 200X	Particulars	Fo.	Totals	Date 200X	Particulars	Fo.	Totals
Mar 31	H. Baker	SL2	200.00	Mar 31	Profit and Loss	NL27	200.00

p19   p19

Provision for Doubtful Debts Account

Date	Particulars	Fo.	Totals	Date 200X	Particulars	Fo.	Totals
				Mar 31	Profit and Loss	NL27	600.00

p27   p27

Profit and Loss Account

Date 200X	Particulars	Fo.	Totals	Date 200X	Particulars	Fo.	Totals
Mar 31	Provision for Doubtful Debts	NL19	600.00				
31	Bad Debts	NL20	200.00				

Fig. 71. Accounting for bad and doubtful debts in the ledger.

42 Accounting for bad and doubtful debts

Not every credit customer (or other debtor) will pay what he owes. He may dispute the amounts; some may disappear or go out of business. The debts they owe to the business may be bad, or of doubtful value. If so, our accounts must reflect the fact.

Accounting for bad and doubtful debts, like depreciation, means estimating an erosion of value. But it differs from depreciation because there it is time that erodes the value. Here it is more a product of fate. We can predict what effect age will have on physical assets like motor cars, but we cannot very easily predict which, and how many, debtors won't pay their bills. If we could, we should never have given them credit in the first place! There are no special calculation techniques for bad and doubtful debts as there are in depreciation. You just need to choose a suitable overall percentage, and make specific adjustments from time to time in the light of experience.

Postings

We may know a debt has become worthless because the individual has gone bankrupt, or a company has gone into liquidation. Such a debt must then be posted to a 'bad debts account'. This is an account for specific debts we know to be bad. This is quite aside from our provision for a percentage of debtors control account going bad. If bad debts are recovered later on, we will treat them as credits to bad debts account, and a debit to cash account. We do not need to reopen the individual debtor account, since the posting would result in its immediate closure anyway.

Only if a firm is in liquidation, or if an individual has too few assets to be worth suing, do we need to write off his debt to bad debts account. If the non-payer does have sufficient funds, the firm may be able to sue him successfully for the debt.

Saving tax and being realistic

The reason we need to write down bad or doubtful debts is twofold. First, the firm will be charged income tax on its profits; if the profit figure is shown without allowing for the cost of bad and doubtful debts it will be higher than it should rightly be, and the firm will end up paying more tax than it needs to.

Secondly, the balance sheet should show as realistically as possible the value of the assets of the business. After all, interested parties such as bankers, investors and suppliers will rely on it when making decisions about the firm. Failure to write off bad debts, and too little provision for doubtful debts, will mean an unrealistically high current asset of debtors being shown.

JOURNAL

200X	Particulars	Fo.	Debit	Credit
Aug 30	Bad Debts	NL9	200.00	
	H. Baker	SL5		200.00
	To write off bad debt.			

---

p5
SALES LEDGER
H. Baker

Dr.							Cr.
200X				200X			
Aug 1	Balance	b/d	200.00	Aug 30	Bad Debts	NL9	200.00

---

p9
NOMINAL LEDGER
Bad Debts

Dr.					Cr.
200X				200X	
Aug 30	H. Baker	SL5	200.00		

Fig. 72. Worked example of bad debt accounting (1).

1. Suppose A. Frazer received information on 30 August that H. Baker, a customer who owed the firm £200, had been declared bankrupt; the appropriate entries in the books would be as shown in Figure 72.

JOURNAL

200X	Particulars	Fo.	Debit	Credit
Mar 31	Profit & Loss	NL30	600.00	
	Provision for Doubtful Debts	NL20		600.00
	To provide for doubtful debts			

LEDGER

NL20   *Provision for Doubtful Debts*

Dr.			Cr.	
200X		200X		
		Mar 31	Profit & Loss	600.00

NL30   *Profit and Loss*

Dr.			Cr.
200X		200X	
Mar 31	Provision for Doubtful Debts	600.00	

Fig. 73. Worked example of Provision for Doubtful Debts (2).

2. Suppose that A. Frazer estimates his necessary bad debts provision for the year ending 31 March as £600; the book-keeping entries would be as shown in Figure 73.

43 Accounting for bad and doubtful debts step-by-step

Posting to 'provision for doubtful debts account' and 'bad debts account'

You will need:
- the journal
- the nominal ledger
- the sales ledger.

Step-by-step

1. Decide the percentage figure and from that the actual amount you will use as a provision for doubtful debts (e.g. 1% or 2%).

2. Write in the next available space in the journal the date (in the date column) and the words 'Profit and loss account' in the particulars column.

3. Enter the value of your provision in the debit cash column.

4. Beneath the last entry in the particulars column, indenting slightly, write: 'Provision for doubtful debts'.

5. Enter the same value in the credit cash column.

6. Repeat the process when writing off any actual bad debts, but in this case you need to debit the bad debts account and credit the individual debtor accounts.

7. Now post to the nominal and sales ledger, exactly following the instructions you have just written in the journal.

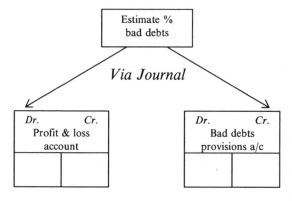

44 Partnership accounts

It is now time to change perspective. We are no longer dealing with pieces of the accounting system, but with different types of accounts for different purposes, beginning with accounts for partnerships. Partnership accounts differ from sole proprietor accounts in two ways:

- a profit and loss appropriation account is needed and

- separate capital accounts are needed for each partner.

In every other way, they are the same.

What is a partnership?

Partnerships are business units owned jointly by more than one person. Such people may have joined in partnership for all kinds of reasons. Perhaps neither had enough capital on their own; perhaps they wished to obtain economies of scale by combining their capitals; perhaps they had matching skills or matching control of the factors of production (e.g. one owned land and buildings while the other had special skills). There are partnerships of solicitors, accountants, building contractors, agencies—in fact of almost any kind of business activity.

Each partner is responsible 'jointly and severally' for all the debts of the partnership. This means that if the business cannot pay its debts, the creditors can hold each and every partner personally responsible. More than that, if one partner has personal assets such as a house and savings, while the other partners have none, creditors can sue the partner who does have assets for all the debts of the partnership—not just for his 'share' of the debts.

There are endless types of financial arrangement in partnerships. For example profits may be shared in proportion to capital invested; or interest may be paid on capital before any residual net profit is shared equally, regardless of capital. Similarly, the partners may agree that interest will be charged on all individual drawings against capital. At the onset, they may decide that each working partner will receive a fixed salary. It is to take care of all such points that partnership accounts have these extra facilities.

Where there is no written partnership agreement, the Partnership Act 1890 (section 24) states that no interest is to be allowed on capital except where provided in excess of any agreement (in which case 5% would be allowed). No interest is to be charged on drawings; no partner will be entitled to a salary, and each will share the profits equally.

45 Partnerships: appropriation accounts

The appropriation account is just an extension of the trading, profit & loss account. In it, we post the appropriation (i.e. sharing out) of net profit between the partners. We do not need an appropriation account in the accounts of a sole proprietor, because all the net profit goes to the one proprietor's capital account. In a partnership or limited company, things are a little more complicated.

- In a partnership some of the profit may be owed to the partners for interest on capitals they have invested.

- If a partner has drawn money from the business (other than salary) he may have to pay interest on it, according to arrangements between the parties. Any such interest payment will have to be deducted from any interest due to him on his capital. We show such transactions in the appropriation account.

- If a partner has lent money to the partnership, however, that is a very different thing. Any interest payable to that partner would be an expense to the business, not an appropriation of profit. It's proper place would be in the profit & loss account.

After deducting these items from the net profit (brought down from the profit & loss account) we have to show how the rest of the profit will be shared out. We will show an equal split, or an unequal one, depending on the profit-sharing arrangements between the partners.

What you need:
- the ledger
- details of interest rate on capital due to partners
- details of interest rate payable by partners on drawings
- details of partners' capitals
- details of partners' drawings
- details of partners' salaries and/or fees
- details of profit-sharing arrangements.

Preparation
Work out the interest on capital due to each partner. Remember to apply the correct percentage interest rate. Work out the interest payable by each partner on his drawings, again applying the correct percentage interest rate.

FRAZER AND BAINES
PROFIT AND LOSS APPROPRIATION ACCOUNT
for year ended 31 December 200X

Net Profit b/d				21,000
Interest on Capital (10%)		Interest on drawings (12%)		
Frazer	2,000	Frazer	240	
Baines	5,000	Baines	300	540
Salary: Frazer	8,000	15,000		
Share of Residual Profits				
Frazer (67%)		2,180		
Baines (33%)		4,360		
		21,540		21,540

Vertical Format

Profit & Loss Appropriation Account of Frazer and Baines

Net Profit b/d			21,000
Frazer			
Interest on Capital (10%)	2,000		
Less interest on drawings (12%)	240		
	1,760		
Salary	8,000	9,760	
Baines			
Interest on Capital (10%)	5,000		
Less interest on drawings (12%)	300	4,700	
Share of profits in ratio 2:1			
Frazer	2,180		
Baines	4,360	6,540	21,000
			00,000

Fig. 74. Worked examples of partnership accounts.

46   Partnership accounts step-by-step

Step-by-step

1. Make another heading under the completed profit & loss account in the ledger: 'Profit & loss appropriation account.'

2. Bring down the net profit from the profit & loss account.

3. In the credit column record: 'Interest payable on drawings' for each partner, marking it accordingly.

4. In the debit column enter: 'Interest on Capitals' for each partner, marking each entry accordingly.

5. In the debit column record the value of individual partners' salaries, marking each one accordingly.

6. Again in the debit column, record the individual profit shares of each partner, marking each one accordingly. Show the proportion, e.g. ½ or a percentage e.g. 50%.

7. Total up and balance this 'account' (the balance c/d will be zero).

Converting final accounts into vertical format
You can now rewrite your final accounts in a more useful vertical format. If you do, change the appropriation account in the same way. The figure opposite (bottom) shows how this is done.

The figure opposite (top) shows an alternative, horizontal layout, but remember that vertical formats are much more popular in Britain and you should use them in exams and in business unless told otherwise.

Example: Frazer and Baines
Frazer and Baines are partners. Frazer initially invested £20,000 in the business and Baines £50,000. Frazer took drawings of £2,000 during the year and Baines £2,500. It had been agreed at the onset that 10% interest would be paid on capitals, interest of 12% would be payable on drawings and that Frazer, because he, alone, would be working full-time in the business, would receive a salary of £8,000. Suppose, also, that the net profit shown in the Profit and Loss Account at the end of the current year is £21,000. Following the step-by-step instruction given here, the examples opposite show what the Appropriation Account might look like.

Before amalgamation   **A. FRAZER**
BALANCE SHEET
as at 28 February 200X

FIXED ASSETS			
Workshop and Yard			45,000
Machinery	4,000		
Less Provision for Depreciation	200	3,800	
Motor Van	6,000		
Less Provision for Depreciation	2,000	4,000	7,800
Goodwill			5,800
			58,600
CURRENT ASSETS			
Stock of materials	4,500		
Debtors	1,200		
Cash at Bank	150		
	5,850		
Less CURRENT LIABILITIES			
Creditors	5,100		
Working Capital			750
TOTAL ASSETS			59,350
Financed by:			
CAPITAL as at 1 March 200X			57,050
Add Profit			11,300
			68,350
Less Drawings			9,000
TOTAL LIABILITIES			59,350

Before amalgamation   **E. BAINES**
BALANCE SHEET
as at 28 February 200X

FIXED ASSETS		
Machinery	3,000	
Less Provision for Depreciation	150	2,850
Motor Lorry	5,000	
Less Provision for Depreciation	1,000	4,000
Goodwill		2,000
		8,850
CURRENT ASSETS		
Stock of materials	900	
Debtors	4,000	
Cash at Bank	41,000	
Cash in Hand	500	
	46,400	
Less CURRENT LIABILITIES		
Creditors	2,600	
Working Capital		43,800
TOTAL ASSETS		52,650
Financed by:		
CAPITAL as at 1 March 200X		42,450
Add Profit		10,200
TOTAL LIABILITIES		52,650

Fig. 75. Two balance sheets before amalgamation
into a partnership.

47 Amalgamating sole proprietorships into a partnership

Consolidation

Now we come to a new accounting technique, **consolidation**. The idea is to consolidate or amalgamate the accounts of two separate businesses into those of a single partnership. The method is very simple:

- we just add each of the individual balance sheet items together, after making adjustments in each for any changes in asset values agreed by the parties.

Making the adjustments

Such adjustments may arise for example because A thinks his 'provision for bad debts' of 5% is reasonable, while B feels it should be 7½%; or B might feel that one of A's machines is not worth what A's balance sheet says it is; and so on. If the amalgamation is to go ahead, the parties will have to settle all such disagreements first.

When we make such adjustments, it is bound to affect the capital figure. So we also need to make the adjustment to the capital accounts, before consolidating the balance sheets by adding all their components together. Indeed, if we didn't adjust the capital accounts, the individual balance sheets would cease to balance, and then the consolidated one would not balance either.

The 'goodwill' value of each business

The parties may agree that different values of **goodwill** existed in their businesses before amalgamation. Perhaps one business was long-established, while the other one was rather new and had not yet built such a good reputation. In such a case, each business would write an agreed figure for goodwill into its balance sheet before amalgamation. It would post the other side of the dual posting to the credit of its capital account. On amalgamation we then add the two goodwill amounts together, just like all the other assets.

Writing off goodwill after amalgamation

If it is decided later on to write it off, the one aggregated goodwill figure in the post-amalgamation accounts will be credited to goodwill account; the debit entry to complete the dual posting will be posted to the partners' current accounts, in proportion to their profit-sharing arrangements (unless a different agreement exists between them).

FRAZER AND BAINES
BALANCE SHEET
as at 1 March 200X

FIXED ASSETS

Yard and Workshop	45,000
Machinery	6,650
Motor Van	4,000
Motor Lorry	4,000
Goodwill	7,800
	67,450

CURRENT ASSETS

Stock of Materials	5,400	
Debtors	5,200	
Cash at Bank	41,150	
Cash in Hand	500	
	52,250	

Less CURRENT LIABILITIES

Creditors	7,700	
Working Capital		44,550
TOTAL ASSETS		112,000

Financed by:
CAPITAL ACCOUNTS

Frazer	59,350
Baines	52,650
	112,000

Fig. 76. Opening balance sheet of the new partnership.

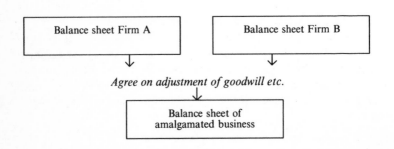

48   How to consolidate two balance sheets

On the previous pages we saw that, to amalgamate two busineses into one, we have to consolidate (add together) their two balance sheets. It is quite a simple procedure.

What you need:

- the two balance sheets

- details of any changes (adjustments) to the item values, as agreed between the owners of the two businesses.

Step-by-step

1. Adjust any item values as appropriate, in other words correct the amounts from their original values to the new agreed values.

2. Take care to amend the capital values, too, so that the individual balance sheets do, in fact, still 'balance'.

3. Add together the values of each item (other than depreciation). Then write out a consolidated balance sheet for the new partnership.

Note on depreciation
Provision for depreciation is not carried over into the new partnership, because the business unit has in effect purchased the assets at their already written down value.

Example
On the facing page we can see the consolidated balance sheet of the businesses of Frazer and Baines (their separate balance sheets were shown on page 112). Notice how the newly amalgamated partnership treats the machinery, motor van and motor lorry. The consolidated value of the machinery is £6,650, representing £3,800 (its written down value in Frazer's balance sheet) plus £2,850 (its written down value in Baines' balance sheet).

CERTIFICATE OF INCORPORATION

OF A PRIVATE LIMITED COMPANY

No.

I hereby certify that

is this day incorporated under the Companies Act 1985

as a private company and that the Company is limited.

Given under my hand at the Companies Registration Office,

Cardiff the

an authorised officer

HC002A

Fig. 77. Certificate of Incorporation of a Limited Company.

49   Limited companies

Public and private companies

The form and extent of the accounts of limited companies are
governed by the Companies Act 1985.

There are two main types of limited company:

- **public** limited companies, which have Plc after their name; and

- **private** limited companies, which have Ltd after their name.

Public companies have to disclose more information than private
companies.

The company as a 'person'

The main difference between the company and other business entities
is that it is a legal entity or 'person' quite separate from the
shareholders. The partnership and the sole proprietorship on the
other hand are inseparable from the people involved: if these two
businesses cannot pay their debts then the partners or proprietors
may be called upon to settle them personally, because 'the business's
debts' are in reality 'their debts'. On the other hand a company's
debts are its debts alone. The shareholders cannot be called upon to
settle the company's debts: their liability is limited to the original
value of their shares. In law, a company is a separate legal 'person'
(though obviously not a human one), and so has its own rights and
obligations under the law.

Share capital

Companies' capital
The capital account has its own special treatment in limited company accounts. The capital of limited companies is divided into shares, which people can buy and sell. A share in the capital of the company entitles the shareholder to a share of the profits of the company—just as a partner owning capital in a firm is entitled to profits.

Ordinary and preference shares
There is, however, a difference, because limited companies can have different kinds of shares with different kinds of entitlements attached to them, e.g. **ordinary shares**, and **preference** shares.

- Preference shares receive a fixed rate of dividend (profit share), provided sufficient profit has been made. For example it might be 10% of the original value of the preference shares.

- Ordinary shares have no such limit on their dividend, which can be as high as the profits allow. However, they come second in the queue, so to speak, if the profit is too little to pay dividends to both the preference and ordinary shareholders.

Furthermore, a company is allowed to retain part of the profits to finance growth. How much, is up to the directors. Unless otherwise stated in the company's memorandum of association, preference shares are cumulative, in other words any arrears of dividend can be carried forward to future years until profits are available to pay them. Since the Companies Act 1985, a company is allowed to issue redeemable shares, preference and ordinary. These are shares that the company can redeem (buy back) from the shareholder at his request.

Debentures
Some of the net assets of a company may be financed by debentures. These are loans, and interest has to be paid on them. Since debentures have to be repaid, we have to show them as liabilities in the balance sheet.

50 Limited companies' books and accounts

The profit & loss appropriation account
The appropriation of net profit has to be shown in company accounts, so we need to draw up a **profit & loss appropriation account**. This shows how much of the profit is being set aside for taxation, how much is being distributed in dividends on shares, and how much is being retained in the company for future growth.

A limited company's statutory 'books'
The law requires a company to keep the following books, as well as its books of account:

- a register of members (shareholders)

- a register of charges (liabilities such as mortgages and debentures)

- a register of directors and managers

- a minutes book.

Annual audit
It also requires it to appoint an external **auditor**. This person is an accountant, not employed by the company, who checks that the entries in the accounts are all correct, and that the accounts give a 'true and fair view' of the company.

Special points on company accounts
Limited company accounts differ from those of other business units in several other ways. For sole proprietors and partners, the profit & loss account is closed each year by transferring any balance to capital account. In the case of limited companies, any undistributed profits stay on the profit & loss account as **reserves** along with undistributed profits for all previous periods. However, to avoid showing a high profit & loss account balance, a company will often transfer some of it to a **general reserve account**, when compiling the profit & loss account. These reserves, along with paid up shares, are called **shareholders' funds** because they are owned by the shareholders.

In the balance sheet of a limited company creditors have to be analysed into those falling due for payment within a year, and those falling due in more than a year (e.g. long term loans).

Format 1

1. Turnover
2. Cost of sales
3. Gross profit or loss
4. Distribution costs
5. Administrative expenses
6. Other operating income
7. Income from shares in group companies
8. Income from shares in related companies
9. Income from other fixed asset investments
10. Other interest receivable and similar income
11. Amounts written off investments
12. Interest payable and similar charges
13. Tax on profit or loss on ordinary activities
14. Profit or loss on ordinary activities after taxation
15. Extraordinary income
16. Extraordinary charges
17. Extraordinary profit or loss
18 Tax on extraordinary profit or loss
19. Other taxes not shown under the above items
20. Profit or loss for the financial year

Format 2

1. Turnover
2. Change in stocks of finished goods and in work in progress
3. Own work capitalised
4. Other operating income
5. (a) Raw materials and consumables
   (b) Other external charges
6. Staff costs:
   (a) wages and salaries
   (b) social security costs
   (c) other pension costs
7. (a) Depreciation and other amounts written off tangible and intangible fixed assets
   (b) Exceptional amounts written off current assets
8. Other operating charges
9. Income from shares in group companies
10. Income from shares in related companies
11. Income from other fixed asset investments
12. Other interest receivable and similar income
13 Amounts written off investments
14. Interest payable and similar charges
15. Tax on profit or loss on ordinary activities
16. Profit or loss on ordinary activities after taxation
17. Extraordinary income
18. Extraordinary charges
19. Extraordinary profit or loss
20. Tax on extraordinary profit or loss
21. Other taxes not shown under the above items
22. Profit or loss for the financial year

Fig. 78. Profit & loss account formats under the 1985 Companies Act.

51 Format of company accounts

The Companies Act 1985 gives four alternative layouts for the profit & loss account (two horizontal and two vertical) and two for the balance sheet (one horizontal and one vertical). The choice is up to the directors, but must not then be changed without good and stated reasons. Vertical layouts are the most popular in the UK, so it is those we will deal with here. Remember, though, that the trading, profit & loss account is first of all a ledger account, so it inevitably starts out in horizontal format. When we are ready to distribute it, inside or outside the firm, we can rewrite it in the more popular vertical format. The two alternative vertical formats laid down by the Companies Act 1985 are shown opposite.

Turnover and cost of sales
Turnover means sales. Cost of sales is found by adding purchases and opening stock, plus carriage inwards costs, and deducting the value of closing stock.

Distribution costs
Includes costs directly incurred in delivering the goods to customers.

Administration expenses
Includes such things as wages, directors' remuneration, motor expenses (other than those included in distribution costs), auditor's fees, and so on.

Other operating income
This means all income other than from the firm's trading activities, *eg* income from rents on property or interest on loans.

Directors' report
A Directors' report must accompany all published accounts. 'Small' companies, however, are exempt from filing one with the Registrar of Companies; also they only have to file a modified version of their balance sheet, and do not have to file a profit & loss account at all. Medium-sized companies also have some concessions, in that a modified form of profit & loss account and accompanying notes is allowed.

Internal accounts
Internal accounts or management accounts are those prepared only for use within the company. Unlike published accounts, they are not required by law to be set out in a certain way. However, it pays to keep them as consistent as possible with the published accounts, so that the latter can be drawn up just by adapting the internal accounts slightly.

TRIAL BALANCE
as at 31 December 200X

Sales		308,000
Opening stock	·15,000	
Purchases	180,000	
Closing stock	18,000	18,000
Wages	22,000	
Auditors fees	5,000	
Motor expenses	7,000	
Heat and light	7,000	
Postage	1,500	
Stationery	4,000	
Interest	900	
Depreciation	4,500	
Bad debts	3,500	
Freehold premises	103,400	
Fixtures and fittings	10,000	
Provision for depreciation on fixtures and fittings		500
Motor lorry	10,000	
Provision for depreciation on motor lorry		2,000
Machinery	40,000	
Provision for depreciation on machinery		2,000
Debtors and creditors	48,700	22,500
Cash at bank	19,850	
Cash in hand	50	
Opening balance of profit and loss account		23,400
Accruals		4,000
Share capital: Ordinary shares		90,000
Preference shares		30,000
	500,400	500,400

Fig. 79. A trial balance drawn up in readiness for final accounts.

TRADING PROFIT AND LOSS ACCOUNT
For year ended December 31 200X

		Sales	308,000
Opening Stock	15,000	Closing stock	18,000
Purchases	180,000		
Balance c/d	131,000		
	326,000		326,000
		Gross profit b/d	131,000
Wages	22,000		
Auditors fees	5,000		
Motor expenses	7,000		
Heat and light	7,000		
Postage	1,500		
Stationery	4,000		
Depreciation	4,500		
Bad debts	3,500		
Interest	900		
Balance c/d	75,600		
	131,000		131,000

Profit and Loss Appropriation Account

Provision for taxation	32,000	Net profit b/d	75,600
Proposed dividend		Profit and loss account	23,400
Preference shares	4,500	b/f from last year	
Ordinary shares	30,000		
Profit and loss a/c balance c/f to next year	32,500		
	99,000		99,000

Fig. 80. See how the various balances listed in the trial balance are used to produce the trading, profit & loss account. Page 124 shows this horizontal format converted to the more useful vertical one.

52 Revenue accounts of limited companies

A ledger account
Remember, the trading, profit & loss account is first and foremost a ledger account, and the appropriation account a division of it. So we should begin by treating it as such. Suppose we have all the accounting information ready in the trial balance: this is how we would go about preparing the final accounts.

What you need
- the ledger (all divisions)
- the journal
- the trial balance
- details of end of year adjustments.

Compiling company final accounts step-by-step
Turn back to page 85 and see the tips for preparatory work before you put together the final accounts. Remember to alter your trial balance to take account of adjustments, and to label each item in it according to where it will end up in the trading (T), profit & loss (P) account, or balance sheet (B).

1. Journalise the ledger postings exactly according to the labelling you have just written on the trial balance. In other words, post each item labelled 'T' to the trading account and each item labelled 'P' to the profit & loss account. Post them all to the same side of such accounts (debit or credit) as those on which they appear in the trial balance. The other side of the posting, of course, goes to the account from which they are being transferred. (If you are in doubt about how to journalise, see page 87.)

2. When you have entered all the ledger postings, write beneath them: 'To close revenue and expense accounts and transfer balances to the trading, profit & loss account'.

3. Now post to the trading account, following exactly the instructions you have just written in the journal.

4. Total up and balance the trading account. Bring the balance down to the profit & loss account, as 'gross profit b/d'.

5. Now post to the profit & loss account, following exactly the instructions you have just written in the journal.

ARMSTRONG ENGINEERING LTD
TRADING, PROFIT AND LOSS ACCOUNT
For year ended 31 December 200X

Turnover		308,000
Less Cost of Sales		
Stock as at 1 January 200X	15,000	
Add purchases	180,000	
	195,000	
Less Stock as at 31 December 200X	18,000	177,000
Gross Profit b/d		131,000
Less Administration Expenses:		
Wages	22,000	
Auditors Fees	5,000	
Motor Expenses	7,000	
Heat and Light	7,000	
Postage	1,500	
Stationery	4,000	
Depreciation	4,500	
Bad Debts	3,500	54,500
		76,500
Less Interest Payable:		
Loans Payable within 5 Years		900

Profit and Loss Appropriation Account

Net Profit b/d		75,600
Less Provision for Taxation		32,000
Net Profit After Taxation		43,600
Add Profit and Loss Account		
Balance b/f from Last Year		23,400
		67,000
Less Proposed Dividends:		
Preference Shares	4,500	
Ordinary Shares	30,000	34,500
Profit and Loss Account		
Balance c/f to Next Year		32,500

Fig. 81. A simple example of the profit & loss account, and profit & loss appropriation account, shown on page 122, converted to the more useful vertical format for use within the company.

ARMSTRONG ENGINEERING LTD
TRADING, PROFIT & LOSS ACCOUNT
AND PROFIT AND LOSS APPROPRIATION ACCOUNT
For year ended 31 December 200X

Turnover	308,000
Cost of sales	177,000
Gross Profit	131,000
Administration expenses	54,500
	76,500
Interest payable	900
Profit on ordinary activities before taxation	75,600
Tax on profit from ordinary activities	32,000
Profit on ordinary activities after taxation	43,600
Profit & loss account balance	
Undistributed profits b/f from last year	23,400
	67,000
Proposed dividends	34,500
Undistributed profits c/f to next year	32,500

Fig. 82. The same profit and loss account converted for publication.

6. Open an appropriation account immediately below the profit & loss account (see page 119).

7. Total up and balance the profit & loss account. Bring the balance down as 'Net Profit b/d'.

8. In the credit column, record the profit & loss account balance brought forward from last year.

9. In the debit column, record the figure for provision for taxation. Note: the calculation of corporation tax is beyond the scope of this book; the figure used in the example is rather arbitrary.

10. In the debit column, record the value of 'Proposed Dividends on Shares'.

11. Balance off the account. Write against the balance: 'Profit & Loss Account Balance c/f to next year'.

Worked example
See page 122 for a worked example of posting to the trading, profit & loss acount in the ledger of a limited company using the information given in the trial balance.

Transfer to general reserve
The directors of a company may not wish to show a high profit & loss account balance, because shareholders may demand a higher dividend as a result. Instead they may transfer part of it to General Reserve. Such a transfer would be an additional debit posting in the profit & loss appropriation account, thereby reducing the profit & loss account balance carried forward to the next year.

BALANCE SHEET
as at 31 December 200X

	Cost	Less Provision for Depreciation	Net Book Value
Fixed assets			
Premises	103,400		103,400
Fixtures and Fittings	10,000	500	9,500
Machinery	40,000	2,000	38,000
Motor lorry	10,000	2,000	8,000
	163,400	4,500	158,900
Current assets			
Stock		18,000	
Debtors		48,700	
Cash at Bank		19,850	
Cash in Hand		50	
		86,600	
Less Creditors			
Amounts Falling Due Within			
1 Year	22,500		
Accruals	4,000		
Proposed Dividends	34,500	61,000	
Net Current Assets			25,600
Total Net Assets			184,500
Provision for Liabilities and Charges			
Taxation			32,000
Shareholders Funds			
Authorised Share capital			
100,000 Preference Shares of £1	100,000		
100,000 Ordinary Shares of £1	100,000		
	200,000		
Issued Share Capital			
30,000 Preference Shares of £1		30,000	
90,000 Ordinary Shares of £1		90,000	
		120,000	
Capital and Reserves			
Profit and loss Account Balance		32,500	152,500
			184,500

Fig. 83. An example of a limited company's balance sheet suitable for publication using the information given in the trial balance on page 122.

53 Balance sheets of limited companies

No ledger posting needed

The balance sheet is not a ledger account, so there is no ledger posting to do. We simply draw up a statement showing the balances left on the ledger after we have compiled the trading, profit & loss account. Using the trial balance on page 122 we will compile a balance sheet for internal use, that also meets the requirements of the Companies Act 1985 (Format 1).

Compiling a company balance sheet step-by-step

1. Make a heading: 'Fixed Assets'. Allocate three cash columns on the right of a sheet of paper, and head them 'Cost', 'Less provision for Depreciation', and 'Net Book Value'. Underneath, record the values for each fixed asset. Net book value means value after depreciation. On the left write against each the name of the asset concerned. Total up each column and cross cast (cross check).

2. Make a heading: 'Current Assets'. Enter in the second column the value of stock then write against it on the left: 'Stock'. Beneath the figure enter the value of debtors, and write against it on the left: 'Debtors'. In the second column list the values of the other current assets. On the left write against each the name of the current asset concerned. Total up this column.

3. Make a heading: 'Less Creditors'. In the first column list the values of creditors and accruals relating to this category. On the left, against each, write the names of each class, (i) 'Amounts falling due within one year' and '(ii) Accruals'. Total up this column. Place the total in the second column below the total for current assets.

4. Subtract the total current liabilities (creditors) from the total current assets. Place the total in the third column below the total net book value for fixed assets. You need to place it below the level of the last total because there is an important phrase to be written against this subtotal: 'Net Current Assets' (in other words 'Working Capital'). Add the two totals in the third column and write against that sum: 'Total Net Assets'. If there were any long term creditors (falling due after one year) we would now list them, but in our data there are none.

5. Make a heading: 'Provision for Liabilities and Charges'. Beneath it make a sub-heading 'Taxation'. In the third column record the value of the provision for taxation and write against it: 'Taxation'.

6. Make a subheading: 'Shareholders' Funds'.

7. Underneath that make a subordinate sub-heading, 'Authorised share capital'.

8. In the first cash column list the total authorised value of each class of share, annotating accordingly, e.g. 'Preference Shares of £1', 'Ordinary Shares of £1'.

9. Total up this column and rule it off with a double line.

10. Make a sub-heading: 'Issued Share Capital'. In the second column enter the total value of shares issued in each class of share capital, annotating each, e.g. 'Preference Shares of £1', 'Ordinary Shares of £1'.

11. Total up this column.

12. Make a heading: 'Capital and Reserves'. In the second column, list the profit & loss account balance. Add the last two figures in the second column, i.e. total issued share capital and profit & loss account balance, and place the total in the third column. Add the last two figures in the third column to arrive at the second major total, which must balance with the first (total net assets). There is room for variation in the use of columns. It depends on how many items you need to deal with in each group. But the objectives are clarity and simplicity.

54 Going limited

Three methods of 'going limited'

A sole proprietor or partnership may wish to change the status of its business entity to that of a limited company. If so, it must draw up a balance sheet for the existing business and form a new company to purchase it at an appropriate price. The new company can pay the seller (sole proprietor or partnership) in any of three ways:

1. Buying paid up shares. If the value of the business is say £100,000, then the share capital of the new company will be registered at at least that figure. The seller will transfer his business to the company in exchange for an equal value, not in cash, but in shares.

2. Mixture of shares and debenture. The seller may, on the other hand, wish to accept only part of the payment in shares, and the other part in the form of a debenture. In other words, he would be selling the second part for money—but giving the company time to pay (debentures are a type of secured and usually long-term loan).

3. Selling shares to other parties. Some of the extra cash raised by this means can then be used to buy some of the assets from the former owner (sole proprietor or partnership).

Adjustments to the balance sheet

If outside parties are becoming involved, they may not agree with the various asset values shown in the business's balance sheet. They may for example disagree with the figures for bad debts provision, or with the listed value of stock or goodwill. Adjustments then need to be made to these values to satisfy everyone concerned.

You would need to make a corresponding adjustment to the capital account on the balance sheet of the business before it was bought by the limited company. When all has been agreed, we simply need to record the opening figures in the books of the new company.

There will be two fundamental differences between those entries and the details of the closing balance sheet of the business purchased:

• The capital in the opening balance sheet of the limited company will be analysed into shares (rather than into proprietor's or partners' capital). It will not show the profit or the proprietor's drawings for the period up to the takeover.

• Provision for depreciation will not feature in the opening balance sheet of the new company since it will have purchased the assets at their 'written down value'.

ARMSTRONG ENGINEERING
Balance Sheet as at 31 Mar 200X

INTANGIBLE ASSETS
Goodwill   5,000

FIXED ASSETS
Freehold Premises   35,000
Plant and Machinery   15,000
Less Depreciation   750   14,250

Motor Van   8,000
Less Depreciation   1,600   6,400   55,650
Total Fixed Assets   60,650

CURRENT ASSETS
Stock   9,000
Debtors   10,000
Less Provision for Doubtful Debts   2,000   8,000
Cash at Bank   10,000
Cash in Hand   50
                                                    27,050

Less CURRENT LIABILITIES
Creditors   12,000
Working Capital   15,050
TOTAL ASSETS   75,700

Financed by
CAPITAL
Opening Balance   63,050
Add Profit for Period   19,100
                                                              82,150
Less Drawings   6,450
TOTAL LIABILITIES   75,700

Fig. 84. The balance sheet of Armstrong Engineering before it became
a limited company.

55 Going limited: worked example

Armstrong, a sole proprietor, traded as Armstrong Engineering. He decided to form a limited company and transfer the assets and liabilities to it in return for ordinary shares. Assuming that the creditors had agreed to his transferring to the limited company the responsibility for the debts he had, as a sole proprietor, personally owed to them (by no means always the case), the opening balance sheet of the new company would be as shown below.

ARMSTRONG ENGINEERING LTD		
Balance Sheet as at 31 Mar 200X		
INTANGIBLE ASSETS		
Goodwill		5,000
FIXED ASSETS		
Freehold Premises	35,000	
Plant and Machinery	14,250	
Motor Van	6,400	55,650
Total Fixed Assets		60,650
CURRENT ASSETS		
Stock	9,000	
Debtors	8,000	
Cash at Bank	10,000	
Cash in Hand	50	
	27,050	
Less CURRENT LIABILITIES		
Creditors	12,000	
Working Capital		15,050
		75,700
Financed by		
Authorised Share Capital		
100,000 Ordinary Shares		
@ £1.00 each	100,000	
Issued Share Capital		
75,700 ordinary Shares		
@ £1.00 each		75,700

Fig. 85. The balance sheet of Armstrong Engineering after it became a limited company.

SUBSCRIPTIONS ACCOUNT

200X				200X			
Mar31 Balance	b/d	100		Mar31 Balance	b/d	50	
31 Income and Expenditure account		10,100		Bank		10,100	
31 Balance	c/d	150		Balance	c/d	200	
		10,350				10,350	

Fig. 86. Subscription fees paid by members are usually one of a club's main sources of income. This income is transferred to an 'income & expenditure account'.

Raffle Proceeds	40.00	
Less Expenses	10.00	
Net Proceeds		30.00
Dance Tickets	200.00	
Less Expenses	90.00	
Net Proceeds		110.00
To Income & Expenditure Account		140.00

Fig. 87. A club may also raise income by commercial activities such as raffles and dances. The income from this is also transferred to the income & expenditure account.

56 Club accounts

Here is another variation in format of final accounts. By clubs, we mean here clubs owned by their members, for example political clubs, social clubs and sports clubs. These organisations do not exist to make a 'profit'. All the revenue comes from the shareholders themselves (e.g. as members' subscriptions) and just reflects the cost of the goods and services they consume at the club. Their accounts are a matter of house-keeping, rather than 'trading'; the members contribute to an **accumulated common fund** for the common good.

Surpluses and accumulated funds

Of course, all housekeepers like to 'put a bit by'. Committees of clubs are in effect housekeepers, too, and often develop a small excess of revenue over expenses. But this is not profit: it is merely shareholders' contributions (in various ways) left over after all expenses have been paid. In the accounts it is termed a **surplus**. It is added to the accumulated common fund to be used for the future benefit of members. It is just as an individual may save surplus income to buy things tomorrow which he could not afford today, or to make ends meet if he falls on hard times.

Format of club accounts

Club accounts differ in format from commercial accounts, in just three ways:
- The money we call profit or loss in a partnership, sole proprietorship or limited company, we call a surplus or deficit in a club.
- Instead of a profit & loss account, clubs have an income & expenditure account.
- Instead of a capital account, clubs have an accumulated fund.

That is not to say that no profit-making activities go on in clubs. A club may well run a bar, for example, on commercial lines. If so, a bar trading account is kept, to calculate and record gross profit; bar staff wages appear in the account along with cost of goods sold, as we dealt with on page 81. Any profit is then brought down to the club's income & expenditure account (rather than to a profit & loss account as it would be in a truly commercial business).

You can show other income-generating activities in separate trading accounts (e.g. club shop trading account), but for things like raffle and dance proceeds which do not really involve trading goods, you usually just 'net' the incomes concerned in the income & expenditure account. In other words you set against the income from the sale of tickets the cost of prizes, band hire, and so on.

TRIAL BALANCE
of George Street Social Club
as at 31 March 200X

Opening stock	1,000	
Purchases	30,000	
Bar staff wages	4,500	
Bar Sales		50,000
Staff wages (non-bar)	30,300	
Rent & rates	5,000	
Postage	58	
Telephone	300	
Cleaning	500	
Bank charges	150	
Donations received		2,500
Net dance and concert proceeds		10,000
Subscriptions		5,000
Net raffle and bingo ticket proceeds		500
Commission on fruit machine		4,000
Club premises	62,000	
Fixtures and fittings	10,000	
Provision for depreciation on fixtures and fittings		500
Depreciation	500	
Bar stocks	900	900
Subscriptions in arrear	250	
Cash at bank	2,200	
Cash in hand	50	
Creditors		1,100
Accumulated fund balance as at 1 April 200X		73,208
	147,708	147,708

Fig. 88. Typical trial balance used to prepare a bar trading account and income & expenditure account of a social club.

57 Club accounts: income and expenditure

Preparing final accounts

So far we have considered how to write the final accounts of profit-making organisations including sole-proprietors, partnerships and limited companies. We will now see how to write the final accounts of a non-profit-making organisation, such as a club, or society.

What you need:

- the trial balance
- details of any adjustments to be made to the final accounts
- the journal
- the ledger.

BAR TRADING ACCOUNT

	£		£
Opening Stock	1,000	Sales	50,000
Purchases	30,000	Closing stock	900
Bar Staff Wages	4,500		
Gross Profit c/d	15,400		
	50,900		50,900

INCOME AND EXPENDITURE ACCOUNT

	£		£
Staff Wages (non-Bar)	30,300	Gross Profit b/d from bar	
Rent and Rates	5,000	Trading Account	15,400
Postage	58	Subscriptions	5,000
Telephone	300	Donations Received	2,500
Cleaning	500	Dance and Concert Proceeds	10,000
Bank Charges	150	Raffle and Bingo Tickets	500
Depreciation	500	Commission from Fruit	4,000
Surplus of income over		Machns.	
Expenditure c/d to			
Accumulated Fund	592		
	37,400		37,400

Fig. 89. A bar trading account and an income & expenditure account in the ledger.

135

GEORGE STREET SOCIAL CLUB
BAR TRADING ACCOUNT
for year ended 31 March 200X

Sales			50,000
Add Purchases		30,000	
Opening Stock	1,000		
Less Closing Stock	900	100	
Cost of Goods Sold		30,100	
Add Bar Staff Wages		4,500	34,600
Net Profit c/d to Income and			
Expenditure Account			15,400

INCOME AND EXPENDITURE ACCOUNT

Income	£	£
Gross Profit b/d from Bar Trading Account		15,400
Subscriptions		5,000
Donations Received		2,500
Net dance and Concert Proceeds		10,000
Net raffle and bingo proceeds		500
Commission from Fruit Machine		4,000
		37,400
Less Expenditure		
Staff Wages (non-Bar)	30,300	
Rent and Rates	5,000	
Postage	58	
Telephone	300	
Cleaning	500	
Bank Charges	150	
Depreciation	500	36,808
Surplus of Income over Expenditure		
Transferred to Accumulated Fund		592

Fig. 90. This shows the same account converted to a more useful vertical format. Some clubs may not keep a ledger; if they don't the final accounts would be drawn up directly from the receipts and payments book (the main book of Prime Entry used by club stewards). In such cases there would be no point in preparing them in the ledger format prior to converting them to a more useful form; it would be sensible to use such format from the start. You will, invariably, be asked to prepare final accounts directly from prime sources in exams in this subject, since to go through all the ledger posting stages would take a long time.

58 Club accounts step-by-step

Preparation

First of all, amend the trial balance for any end of year adjustments (if in doubt see page 83). Then, label the destination in the final accounts of each item in the trial balance. For example against 'bar sales' write 'T' for bar trading account; against 'rent & rates' write 'I & E' to show that it will go into the income & expenditure account. Write 'B' beside an asset account for the club's 'motor coach' for example, because you will be listing all assets in the balance sheet.

Bar trading and income and expenditure account step-by-step

1. Turn to the last entry in the journal. Underneath, record the amount of each balance due to go to the bar trading account. Remember to post each one to the same side (debit or credit) as in the trial balance. After each one post the dual aspect of the transaction to the ledger account from which it is being transferred. It is usual to enter each debit value before entering each credit value (see page 45).

2. Immediately below these entries write: 'To close revenue and expense accounts and transfer balances to the bar trading account'.

3. Now record the amount of each balance due to go to the income & expenditure account, remembering after each one to post it to the same side (debit or credit) as it appears in the trial balance. Post the opposite aspect of the transaction to the ledger account from which it is being transferred.

4. Immediately below these entries in the journal, write: 'To close Revenue and Expense Accounts and transfer balances to Income & Expenditure Account'.

5. Now post to the ledger exactly as you have just written in the journal.

6. Total up and balance the bar trading account, and other accounts affected. Bring down the balance of the bar trading account to the Income and Expenditure Account, annotating accordingly.

7. Total up and balance the Income & Expenditure Account and other accounts affected. Against the balance b/d write: 'Surplus of Income over Expenditure [or Deficit of Income to Expenditure] b/d to Accumulated Fund'.

The unused trial balance items make up the Balance Sheet, but that is not a ledger account like the Income and Expenditure Account, so there will be no closing down of ledger accounts and no use of the journal.

GEORGE STREET SOCIAL CLUB

BALANCE SHEET
as at 31 March 200X

FIXED ASSETS

Club Premises		62,000
Fixtures and Fittings	10,000	
Less Depreciation	500	9,500
		71,500

CURRENT ASSETS

Bar Stocks	900	
Subscriptions in arrear	250	
Cash at Bank	2,200	
Cash in hand	50	
	3,400	

Less CURRENT LIABILITIES

Creditors	1,100	
Net Current Assets		2,300
TOTAL NET ASSETS		73,800

Financed by:		
ACCUMULATED FUND		
Balance as at 1 April 200X		73,208
Add Surplus Income Over Expenditure		592
ACCUMULATED FUND BALANCE		
AS AT 31 MARCH 200X		73,800

Fig. 91. Balance sheet of a non-profit making organisation. If done correctly, the two major totals should obviously be equal (in the example above, £73,800). If not, check whether there are any items remaining unticked or uncrossed-out in your trial balance. Check too that you have brought the surplus or deficit down to the balance sheet.

59   The club balance sheet step-by-step

Compiling the club balance sheet step-by-step

1. Head a sheet of paper with the name of the club, and at the top write 'Balance Sheet as at [relevant date]'. Then head three cash columns on the right.
2. Make a heading on the left hand side of the sheet: 'Fixed Assets'.
3. Beneath this in column three, write the value of any premises, e.g. £62,000, and write 'Club Premises' against it on the left.
4. Next, in column two, list the balances of any other fixed assets, in order of permanence. Annotate each one on the far left, for example, 'Fixtures and Fittings'. Beneath each one record the provision for depreciation, writing 'Less Depreciation' and the amount of depreciation, £500 in the example opposite.
5. Subtract the depreciation from each asset, and place the difference in column three (£9,500 in the example).
6. Total up column three.
7. Now make a second main heading, 'Current Assets'.
8. Beneath this in the second cash column write down the balances of the short-life (i.e. current) assets, again in the order of permanence. Write the name of each one, for example Bar Stocks, £900.
9. Total up these balances (in the example £3,400).
10. Now make a third main heading on the left: 'Less Current Liabilities'. Below that, in the first cash column, list the creditors' figure, and the bank overdraft figure if there is one, as shown in the example.
11. Total up this column. Place the total in the second column beneath that for current assets. (If there is only one item you can place it directly into the second column.)
12. Now rule off this column and subtract the latter total from the former. Place the difference in the third column below the total for fixed assets, writing against it: 'Net Current Assets'.
13. Add these two totals and rule off with a double line, writing against it: 'Total Net Assets'.
14. Make a heading below this for 'Financed by Accumulated fund'.
15. Enter the opening accumulated fund balance directly into the third column, writing against it: 'Accumulated fund balance as at [starting date for the accounting period]'.
16. Enter the surplus (or deficit) for the year, annotating it accordingly.
17. Total up the column and rule off with a double line. Annotate the balance: 'Accumulated fund balance as at [date of balance sheet]'.

SUBSCRIPTIONS ACCOUNT

Dr.   *Cr.*

200X				200X			
Mar 31	Prepayments c/d	80.00		Mar 31	Cash Book		630.00
31	Income &			31	Subscriptions		
	Expenditure				in arrear c/d		50.00
	Account	600.00					
			680.00				680.00

200X				200X			
Apr 1	Subscriptions						
	in arrear b/d	50.00		Apr 1	Prepayments b/d		80.00

Fig. 92. Example of a club subscriptions account.

60   Club accounts: adjustments and subscriptions

End of year adjustments
Adjustments such as depreciation, accruals and prepayments apply just as much to non-profit-making clubs as to profit-making organisations, because the aim of accounting is still to record income, expenditure, assets and liabilities as accurately as possible.

Accrued income
Accrued income is dealt with by entering a c/d figure on the credit side of the income account: so the figure you transfer to Income and Expenditure must be higher by the same amount in order to balance the account.

Prepayment
Prepayments are dealt with in the opposite way. You enter them as a c/d figure on the debit side of the account; this will have the opposite effect and make the figure you transfer to the Income and Expenditure Account, lower by that amount.

Each year afterwards we must reverse the adjustments to subscription income accounts. Why?—because some of the receipts posted will represent settlement of those arrears. Also, the prepayment income deducted from last year's account must now be added to this year's, because it is to this year that it properly relates.

Subscriptions
All we have to deal with on subscriptions are:

- prepayments

- subscriptions in arrear

- subscriptions received.

The first two of these are just dealt with as balancing items, i.e. as balances b/d or c/d. They are b/d if they are reversals of last year's adjustments, and c/d if they refer to this year. Whatever figure you then post to balance these two columns is the one you will transfer to the Income and Expenditure Account.

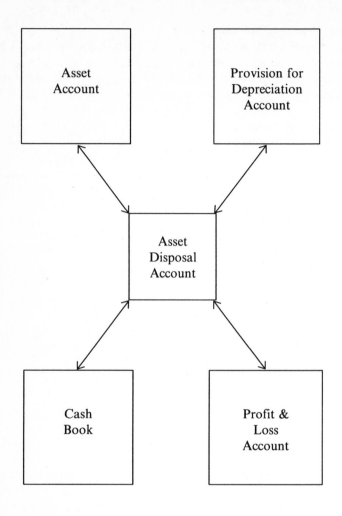

Fig. 93. A schematic illustration of asset disposal. The dual postings with the particular asset account, the account for provision for depreciation on that asset and the cash book take place when the asset is sold. The fourth does not take place until the final accounts are compiled.

61 Asset disposals

A form of final account

Asset disposal accounts are like miniature trading, profit & loss accounts: they are final accounts, and not going on any further. Once written up, with their one and only set of entries, they are balanced and carried down to show the profit or loss on the asset disposal concerned. The account will then remain untouched until such figure is transferred to the profit & loss account. The trading, profit & loss account reports all the revenues and expenses of a business at once. In contrast, asset disposal accounts only report particular transactions, in other words the disposal of individual assets. You write up a separate asset disposal account for each asset disposed of, such as a motor van or machine.

Closing down two related accounts

The idea is not only to record the disposal of the asset, but at the same time to close down the two other accounts which relate to the asset in the books—the 'asset account' itself, and the 'provision for depreciation on asset account'. It both co-ordinates and combines the closing down of these accounts in the way it follows the double entry principle. Otherwise, recording asset disposals would be a messy business, and mistakes would be easily made.

Three pairs of postings

With the asset disposal account you will need to make three pairs of postings:
- transfer the asset concerned from its asset account to your new asset disposal account;
- transfer the provision for depreciation from its own account to your asset disposal account;
- post the sale proceeds to your asset disposal account, with the counterpart posting to cash, bank, or a personal ledger account if sold on credit.

The resulting profit or loss

The balance c/d on the asset disposal account will then represent a profit (if credit) or loss (if debit) on sale of asset. In the end, along with all the other revenue and expense account balances, it will go to the trading, profit & loss account.

JOURNAL

Date 200X	Particulars	Fo.	Dr.	Cr.
Feb 22	Sundries			
	Asset Disposal	NL40	10,000	
	Motor Van	NL20		10,000
	Provision for Depreciation	NL30	6,000	
	Asset Disposal	NL40		6,000
	Bank	CB25	3,000	
	Asset Disposal	NL40		3,000
	To record the disposal of a motor van			

---

p40   **NOMINAL LEDGER**

Asset Disposal Account

200X		Fo.		200X		Fo.	
Feb 22	Motor Van	NL20	10,000	Feb 22	Provision for Depreciation	NL30	6,000
					Bank	CB25	3,000
					Balance c/d		1,000
			10,000				10,000
Feb 23	balance b/d		1,000				

---

p20

Motor Van Account

200X		Fo.		200X		Fo.	
Jan 1	Balance	b/d	10,000	Feb 22	Asset Disposal	NL40	10,000

---

p30

Provision for Depreciation Account

200X		Fo.		200X		Fo.	
Feb 22	Asset Disposal	NL40	6,000	Jan 1	Balance	b/d	6,000

---

p25

CASH BOOK

200X				200X
Feb 22	Asset Disposal	NL40	3,000	

Fig. 94. An example of journalising and ledger posting for an asset disposal (a motor van originally bought for £10,000 and now sold for £3,000).

62 Asset disposals step-by-step

What you will need:
- the nominal ledger
- the journal
- the cash book.

Step-by-step
1. In the next available space in the journal, write the date in the appropriate column, and the word 'Sundries' to indicate a combination posting. Below that write 'Asset Disposal [name of asset]', as in the example opposite.
2. Enter the original value of the asset, i.e. the value actually recorded in the asset account, in the debit cash column (in the example, £10,000).
3. Beneath your heading, indenting slightly, write the name of the asset concerned: 'Motor Van'.
4. Enter the same book value (£10,000) in the credit cash column.
5. Beneath your last entry in the particulars column, write: 'Provision for depreciation on [name of asset]'.
6. In the debit cash column, enter the balance showing on provision for depreciation account, e.g. £6,000.
7. Beneath your last entry in the particulars column, indenting slightly, write the name of the asset disposal account concerned.
8. In the credit cash column, enter the balance of the provision for depreciation account, e.g. £6,000.
9. In the particulars column write 'Cash' or 'Bank' as appropriate (or the name of a personal account if the van was sold on credit).
10. Enter sales proceeds in the debit cash column (e.g. £3,000).
11. Beneath the last entry in the particulars column, indenting slightly, write the name of the asset disposal account concerned.
12. Enter the value of sales proceeds in the credit cash column, e.g. £3,000.
13. Beneath this set of entries write: 'To record disposal of [asset concerned]'.
14. Make postings to the ledger following the instructions you have just recorded in the journal. Open new accounts where necessary (see page 53 if in doubt).
15. Total up and balance the asset account, the provision for depreciation account and the asset disposal acount, the last of which will be the only one which may have a balance remaining. Remember, you need a separate asset disposal account for each asset disposed of.
16. Remember to complete the folio columns.

ERRORS IN ACCOUNTS

1. *Errors of omission*
    A transaction has been missed out altogether.
2. *Errors of commission*
    A transaction has been posted to the wrong account, though to the right side. For example, posted to 'John Smith A/c' instead of 'Colin Smith A/c'.
3. *Compensation errors*
    Different errors of the same value, occurring on the opposite sides of the ledger divisions. The effect of one is obscured by the equal effect of the other, so that the trial balance still balances. There could, in fact, be more than two errors involved, the total debit errors matching the total credit errors.
4. *Errors of principle*
    Where an expense item has been posted to an asset account. Example, a 'Motor Expense' has been posted to 'Motor Car Account'.
5. *Errors of original entry*
    The original entry was wrong. Perhaps the source document, such as an invoice, has been added up wrongly by a sales office clerk, or misread by the book-keeper.
6. *Errors of reversal*
    Both aspects have been posted to the wrong sides: the debit aspect to the credit side, and vice versa.
7. *Posting to the wrong side of the ledger*
    Errors due to the transaction being posted to the wrong side of the ledger.
8. *Omitting one side of dual posting*
    Errors due to complete omission of one side of the dual posting.
9. *Under or over-statement*
    Errors due to under- or overstating one side of the transaction. Example: a gross invoice value, inclusive of VAT, has been posted to an asset or expense account in the ledger.
10. *Errors of summation*
    Sometimes known as 'casting errors'. Columns have been added up wrongly, and the wrong balance carried down.
11. *Errors of transposition*
    A figure has been accidentally reversed. For example 32 has been written as 23, or 414 as 441. This error is always a multiple of 9, and if the error is one of transposition it can be spotted fairly easily.

Fig. 95. Errors in accounts.

63   Correction of errors

The right way to correct errors

No figure should ever be crossed out anywhere in the accounts. If allowed it could hide embezzlement. Of course, genuine mistakes are made, but there is a special way of putting them right. If an error is found it must be recorded in the journal, together with whatever additions or subtractions are needed to the accounts to put matters right.

Types of error

There are 11 types of error, which we can summarise as follows:

Errors of omission

Errors of commission

Compensating errors

Errors of principle

Errors of original entry

Errors of reversal

Errors of posting to the wrong side of ledger

Errors of omitting one side of dual posting

Errors of over/understating one side

Errors of summation ('casting errors')

Errors of transposition

On the opposite page each one is explained in more detail.

Only the last five of these will be shown up by the trial balance failing to balance.

An error of commission, original entry or reversal will become apparent when a customer or supplier, whose account has been wrongly affected, informs you. He will certainly be quick to let you know if the error is to his disadvantage.

JOURNAL			
Date	Particulars	Dr.	Cr.
200X			
April 30	K.Gange	2,000.00	
	Sales		2,000.00
	To correct Error of omission		
30	Heat and Light	400.00	
	Purchases		400.00
	To correct error of principle		
30	S.Jones	90.00	
	Motor Expenses	10.00	
	Cash Sales		100.00
	To correct compensating errors due to Motor Expenses and Cash Sales both being undercast and S. Jones (debit) being omitted.		
30	A. Singer	50.00	
	A. Singh		50.00
	To correct error of commission		
30	Motor Expenses	15.00	
	Edwards Garage		15.00
	To Correct Error of original entry		
30	Depreciation	80.00	
	Provision for Depreciation		80.00
	To correct error of reversal affecting both accounts in the sum of £40.00*		

Fig. 96. Accounting for errors: entries in the journal. Note: if depreciation account has been credited with £40.00, instead of debited, we must debit it with £80.00 and vice versa for provision of depreciation account.

64   Correcting errors step-by-step

Identifying errors
As we saw on page 73, only the following errors will be shown up by the trial balance failing to balance:

- errors of posting one aspect of the transaction to the wrong side of the ledger
- errors of omission of one side of the dual posting
- errors of under- or overstating one side of the transaction
- errors of summation ('casting errors')
- errors of transposition of digits (e.g. 32 written as 23).

Looking for errors in the trial balance step-by-step
1. If the trial balance fails, look for a figure equal to the error amongst all the balances. If such a figure appears once only, its dual posting may have been omitted from the trial balance (though it may also be included in a larger posting), or that figure may have been missed out when summing the column.
2. Next, divide the discrepancy by 2. Look for a figure equal to the quotient of the calculation in the trial balance. If the error is due to something being posted on the wrong side, this will show it up.
3. Check whether the discrepancy is divisible by 9. If it is, it may be due to an error of transposition.
4. Check your addition of the columns.
5. Check that each of the balances in turn have been correctly copied from the ledger accounts.
6. Check the balances of the ledger accounts.

Treatment of minor errors
If an error reflected in the trial balance is small (e.g. £30) and it is hard to trace, it is permissible to add it to current liabilities or current assets under the heading **suspense account** just so that compilation of final accounts can go ahead. But you should never do this when the error is large. When you find the error, correct it in the journal as described (see example on opposite page).

Of course, the true profit or loss figure may be distorted as a result of this error. That is why it is only permissible to handle small errors in this way. When the error is later discovered and corrected, a statement of corrected net profit can be written up to supplement the year's final accounts.

Value Added Tax Return

For the period
01 04 95 to 30 06 95

HM Customs
and Excise

For Official Use

Registration Number   Period
                       06 95

You could be liable to a financial penalty if your completed return and all the VAT payable are not received by the due date.

Due date: 31 07 95

For Official Use

Your VAT Office telephone number is 01752 777123

Before you fill in this form please read the notes on the back and the VAT leaflet *"Filling in your VAT return"*. Fill in all boxes clearly in ink, and write 'none' where necessary. Don't put a dash or leave any box blank. If there are no pence write "00" in the pence column. Do not enter more than one amount in any box.

For official use		£	p
	VAT due in this period on sales and other outputs **1**		
	VAT due in this period on acquisitions from other EC Member States **2**		
	Total VAT due (the sum of boxes 1 and 2) **3**		
	VAT reclaimed in this period on purchases and other inputs (including acquisitions from the EC) **4**		
	Net VAT to be paid to Customs or reclaimed by you (Difference between boxes 3 and 4) **5**		
	Total value of sales and all other outputs excluding any VAT. Include your box 8 figure **6**		00
	Total value of purchases and all other inputs excluding any VAT. Include your box 9 figure **7**		00
	Total value of all supplies of goods and related services, excluding any VAT, to other EC Member States **8**		00
	Total value of all acquisitions of goods and related services, excluding any VAT, from other EC Member States **9**		00

Retail schemes. If you have used any of the schemes in the period covered by this return, enter the relevant letter(s) in this box.

DECLARATION: You, or someone on your behalf, must sign below.

If you are enclosing a payment please tick this box.

I, ...declare that the
(Full name of signatory in BLOCK LETTERS)
information given above is true and complete.

Signature ....Date ....19...........
A false declaration can result in prosecution.

CO 28664-0(0393)   0073887   F 3790 (February 1994)

VAT 100

Fig. 97. Sample VAT Form (VAT 100): Courtesy Controller of HMSO (Crown Copyright).

65 Value Added Tax

A tax on purchases

Value Added Tax (or VAT) is very different from income tax and corporation tax. The last two are claimed at the point of income—VAT is claimed at the point of purchase. Also, a business is a source of taxation for income tax and corporation tax, but for VAT it is simply a kind of collector. A **taxable** firm has to collect VAT on the sale price of all its goods and services from its customers, and pay it over to HM Customs & Excise as **output tax**. Of course, the firm is also a customer of other firms, because it needs to buy goods and services itself. But the VAT it pays on these purchases (**input tax**) can be set against the VAT it has collected from its customers; it only has to pay the balance (difference) to HM Customs & Excise. (If the balance is a negative one, then HM Customs & Excise refund the balance to the firm.) So in the end, it is only private individuals who actually pay VAT—plus firms too small to have to register for VAT (though they can still register if they wish).

VAT rates

There are a number of VAT statuses falling into two main categories:
- exempt
- taxable

In the second category there can be an infinite number of different tax rates applying to different kinds of goods or services. The rate can be zero percent, or any number of positive rates. 'Zero rated' does not mean 'exempt'. They are two different things. For a long time the basic rate was 15%, but from 1991 it was increased to 17½%.

VAT records

There are several ways of keeping VAT records—a basic one used by most types of business, and various special schemes for particular kinds of business. We will consider the basic one first.

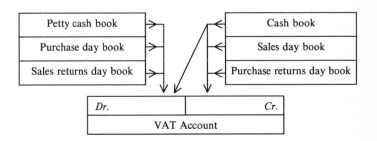

Fig. 98. Sources for the VAT account.

SALES DAY BOOK

Date 200X	Customer	Inv No	Gross Value	Net Zero R (0%)	Net Rate A (8%)	Net Rate B (15%)	VAT	Analysis Columns
Jan 1	S. Jones	59	150.00	150.00				
4	A. Singh	60	540.00	200.36	93.00	208.00	38.64	
			690.00	350.36	93.00	208.00	38.64	

PURCHASE DAY BOOK

Date 200X	Supplier	Inv No	Gross Value	Net Zero R (0%)	Net Rate A (15%)	Net Rate B (8%)	VAT	Analysis columns
Jan 4	Entwhistle	1/01	460.00		400.00		60.00	

PETTY CASH BOOK

p50

Dr.   Cr.

← Analysis Columns →

Amount	Fo.	Date 200X	Particulars	Rcp. No.	Gross Value	Net exempt	Net Rate A	Net Rate B	VAT	Postg.	Stnry
40.00		Jan 1	Balance b/d								
		28	Stamps	1/1	10.00	10.00				10.00	
			Envelopes	1/2	11.50		10.00		1.50		10.00
					21.50	10.00	10.00		1.50	10.00	10.00
21.50	CB8	31	Cash							NL30 NL15	NL117
			Balance c/d		40.00						
61.50					61.50						
40.00		Feb 1	Balance b/d								

LEDGER

p30

NL50

Dr.   VAT   Cr.

200X					1991			
Jan 31	Bought Ledger Control	BL60	60.00	Jan 1	Balance	b/d		30.00
	Petty Cash	PCB50	1.50	31	Sales Ledger Control	SL61		38.64
31	Bank	CB47	7.14					
			68.64					68.64

Note: The entry annotated 'Bank' represents a cheque paid to HM Customs & Excise for the balance payable for the quarter.

Fig. 99. Accounting for VAT: worked example of VAT recordings in daybook, petty cash book and ledger.

66 Accounting for VAT

The prime entries for VAT

The business needs a place to make the prime entries for VAT. This can simply be an extra column or so in the day books (see examples on page 152). In the extra column you separately record the VAT content of purchase invoices (**inputs**) and of sales invoices (**outputs**). The petty cash book, too, can be used to record VAT in the same way; in a special column you can enter the VAT charged on petrol and other small items.

We have already come across this extra column in the day books and the petty cash book earlier on (page 40). From there it is just a matter of posting the extra column to the ledger (i.e. a 'VAT Account' in the ledger) along with others, i.e. the individual, analysed 'Net Amount' columns:

- you post the VAT on purchases to the debit of the VAT account

- you post the VAT on sales to the credit of the VAT account.

You then total up and balance the VAT account, just like any other account in the ledger. The balance represents the tax payable or repayable, depending on whether the firm has collected in more than it has paid out.

Step-by-step

We have already seen how to record VAT step-by-step in the sections on books of prime entry and ledger posting (pages 15 to 55). All tax regardless of the rate, goes into the same column. The net amounts (i.e. net of VAT) in each transaction must be analysed in terms of the tax rate to which they relate. Even zero-rated and exempt goods or services must be treated like this.

You could in theory need any number of net columns in the books of prime entry, but in practice you will probably not need more than three or four.

Special arrangements for retailers

It would be a virtually impossible task for some shops to record every individual sale. Take a sweet shop, for example. It may well sell hundreds of packets of sweets or bars of chocolate a day. The proprietor simply wouldn't be able to record each item individually, so special schemes have been devised for retailers, which excuse them from having to keep itemised VAT records on sales. There are several such schemes, and the retailer chooses one most suited to his kind of business.

67 Incomplete records

'Shoebox jobs'

Sometimes, small businesses neglect their book-keeping in the first
year or two. They find other day-to-day business operations too
demanding. The administrative side of the business seems non-
productive. 'Let's make hay while the sun shines,' they say; 'we'll
catch up with the book-keeping when business is slack'. But often the
accounts are put off, until suddenly the proprietor receives a high
income tax assessment and demand. This comes because the Inland
Revenue has not received his final accounts on which to charge the
correct tax. He is given 30 days to appeal against the assessment; the
appeal will probably be granted, but he will only have a short time to
get his records up-to-date and produce final accounts.

When he begins the task, he finds sales and purchase invoices all
over the place, in no particular date order. Cheque book stubs have
not all been filled in; he cannot find all his old bank statements; there
are screwed up petrol receipts in every pocket of his working clothes
and all corners of his lorry or van. He becomes bewildered, dumps
everything he can find in a box and takes them along to an
accountant. Little wonder accountants call these 'shoebox jobs'.
Invariably some documents have been lost, so normal double entry
book-keeping is impossible. A way has to be found to fill in all the
gaps.

The capital comparison method

One method is to draw up an opening and a closing statement of
affairs, and deduct the opening capital from the closing capital. This
is called the capital comparison method. The idea is to add together
the fixed assets, the merchandise (stock), the accounts receivable
(money owed to the proprietor after bad debt provision), cash in hand
and cash at bank at the date in question. Deduct from that the
accounts payable (money owed by the proprietor) and the difference
will be capital. These statements are in effect the balance sheet,
though the term balance sheet should really only be used when it has
actually been drawn up from the proper ledger 'balances'.

- The difference between the capital at the end of the year, and that
  at the start of the year, is the net profit.

There is one big flaw in using this method alone. Some of the
profit—we do not know how much—may have been taken out by the
proprietor in drawings during the year; so the difference between
opening and closing capitals will not itself necessarily tell us the

profit. Example: suppose the opening capital was £10,000 and the closing capital £11,000. Deducting opening from closing capital suggests a net profit of £1,000. But what if the proprietor had drawn £5,000 during the year? The profit would then really have been £6,000 (£1,000 plus £5,000).

If we have accounts for drawings, however, this problem is resolved. We just add the drawings to the difference between opening and closing capitals to measure the profit.

Capital comparison method step-by-step

Let us see how we might put these statements together. Remember the formula:

Total Assets − Current Liabilities = Total Net Assets

Capital plus long-term liabilities (not payable within the next year) must equal that.

1.   The first part of our closing statement of affairs will give us total net assets. We can complete it from current information, e.g. value of premises, fixtures and fittings, machinery and motor vehicles, stock (counted and valued), debtors, bank balance, cash in hand, and creditors.

2.   The first section of the second half can also be filled in from current information, i.e. the details of any longterm liabilities such as bank loans. We will have to assemble both these sections from whatever evidence is available to us, where the opening statement of affairs is concerned.

3.   We can also fill in the total for the second half of the statement. It will essentially be the same as the total net assets. Provided there are no long-term loans this figure will represent the capital. In our closing statement of affairs we will need to analyse this capital figure to show the net profit. This is found by addition and deduction, filling in the gaps as required. We will know the total: what we need are the figures to get us there. These are the steps in the calculation:

	Example
Opening Capital (from Opening Statement of Affairs)	1,000
Add Capital Injections	Nil
Add Profit	(?)
Less Drawings	4,000
Equals Closing Capital	2,000

If the opening capital was £1,000, closing capital £2,000, no additional capital injections, and drawings of £4,000, then profit must be £5,000 (£1,000 + £0 + £5,000 − £4,000 = £2,000).

ARMSTRONG ENGINEERING
STATEMENT OF AFFAIRS
as at 1 July 200X

FIXED ASSETS

Leasehold Premises			40,000
Fixtures and Fittings			5,000
Motor Vehicle			3,000
			48,000

CURRENT ASSETS

Stock	2,500		
Debtors	1,900	4,400	
Less CURRENT LIABILITIES			
Creditors	2,200		
Bank Overdraft	1,200	3,400	1,000
Total Net Assets			
Represented by Capital			49,000

ARMSTRONG ENGINEERING
STATEMENT OF AFFAIRS
as at 30 June 200X

FIXED ASSETS

Leasehold Premises	40,000		
Less depreciation	2,000		38,000
Fixtures and Fittings	5,000		
Less depreciation	250		4,750
Motor Vehicle	3,000		
Less Depreciation	1,000		2,000
			44,750

CURRENT ASSETS

Stock	3,600		
Debtors	2,900	6,500	
Less CURRENT LIABILITIES			
Creditors	1,800		
Bank Overdraft	100	1,900	
Net Current Assets			4,600
TOTAL NET ASSETS			49,350

Financed by:	
Opening Capital	49,000
Add Profit	*8,550*
Less Drawings	(8,200)
	49,350

Fig. 100. Using the capital comparison method to complete. The profit figure, given in italics, is the only figure which could fulfil the requirements of the sum.

68 Capital comparison method step-by-step

What you need
- Records of assets and liabilities at the start of the accounting period.
- Records of assets and liabilities at the end of the period.
- As many other records as possible for the period in question.

Step-by-step
To draw up the statement of affairs at the start of the accounting period:

1. List the fixed assets in order of permanence, and total.
2. List and total up the current assets (in order of permanence).
3. List and total up the current liabilities.
4. Deduct from last total.
5. Add to the total fixed assets.
6. List any long-term liabilities (other than proprietor's capital) e.g. bank loans, mortgages and leases of more than a year.
7. Enter as capital whatever figure you need to make this column exactly equal the total net assets figure.

Construct, in exactly the same way, a statement of affairs as at the end of the accounting period. Deduct the opening capital from the closing capital. Add any drawings, and deduct any capital injections by the proprietor throughout the year to arrive at the net profit for the year.

The last two steps are usually built into the format of the closing statement of affairs. In the capital section you deduct the opening capital from the closing capital, and record drawings and capital injections when arriving at and displaying the net profit. You construct the statement as far as possible in standard balance sheet format, and then fill in the missing figures by simple arithmetic.

Example
Suppose Armstrong has failed to keep proper accounts during the last year. Faced with a tax demand, he asks us to calculate his profit for the year to 30 June 200X but he can only provide us with the following information: his leasehold premises were worth £40,000 at the start of the year, but have gone down in value by £2,000 since then. He had plant and machinery worth £5,000 which he has not added to; depreciation of £250 is assumed since then. A motor vehicle valued at £3,000 at the start of the year is now worth only £2,000. The stock level has risen from £2,500 to a present level of £3,600, the debtors figure has gone from £1,900 to £2,900. The bank overdraft has gone down from £1,200 to £100 and creditors have gone down

```
Dr.                                                           Cr.
                    TOTAL DEBTORS ACCOUNT

Balance b/d        200.00          Cheques        150.00
Sales              300.00          Balance c/d    350.00
                   500.00                         500.00
```

```
                  TOTAL CREDITORS ACCOUNT

Cash Paid to                       Balance b/d   2,000.00
Suppliers         1,200.00         Purchases     2,200.00
Balance c/d       3,000.00
                  4,200.00                       4,200.00
```

```
                    BANK RECONCILIATION
                    as at 31 December 200X

Balance as per Bank Statement (overdrawn)        7,010.00

Add cheques drawn but not as yet
presented for payment:
     S. Jones                      90.00
     Frazer & Baines              100.00           190.00

Corrected Balance as per Bank Statement          7,200.00
   (overdrawn)
```

```
                    BANK RECONCILIATION
                    as at 31 December 200X

Balance as per Bank Statement (overdrawn)        6,247.00

Add cheques drawn but not as yet
presented for payment:

     A. Singh                      45.00
     Inko                         145.00           190.00

Corrected Balance as per Bank Statement          6,437.00
   (overdrawn)
```

Fig. 101. Opening and closing bank reconciliations.

from £2,200 to £1,800. Furthermore, we know he has taken drawings of £8,200 to live on during the year. Page 156 shows how we would calculate his profit using the capital comparison method.

Additional proof for the taxman

While the calculation of profit based on this method alone may satisfy the proprietor of a small business, the staff at HM Inspector of Taxes are, understandably, likely to require additional proof that the profit figure claimed is accurate. After all, it is asking them to rely 100% on the honesty of the proprietor, not to mention the quality of his memory, in respect of the drawings he has taken.

If we have details of cash and banking transactions, plus accrued debtors and creditors for trading transactions and expenses, we can put together a trading, profit & loss account for the period, and we can use it to prove the figures in the closing statement of affairs. In fact, we could even compile the closing statement of affairs directly from those same sources, with the addition of information from the opening statement of affairs and details of any capital changes and changes in longterm liabilities.

This is how to compile final accounts where many—but not all—the records are available. It involves drawing up:

- opening and closing statements of affairs

- cash and bank account analyses, which itself requires opening and closing bank reconciliations

- total debtors account

- total creditors account

- trial balance

- revenue accounts.

A. FRAZER
BANK ACCOUNT ANALYSIS
for year ended 31 December 200X

Dr.	200X	Particulars	Motor	Wages	Rent	Heat/ Light	Post/ Tel	Drwgs	Spec Items	Cr. Totals
1,200.00	Jan 1	Balance b/d								
	1	Edwards Garage	40.00							40.00
	3	S. Wilson		250.20						250.20
	5	Edwards Garage	310.10							310.10
1,520.00	15	Debtors								
	18	Razi & Thaung			20.70					20.70
	20	A. Morris		31.50						31.50
220.40	27	Entwhistle								
	27	Northern Elec				100.00				100.00
	28	L. Cleaves		30.00						30.00
	31	Cash						400.00		400.00
	31	Brit. Telecom					50.00			50.00
	31	Keele Engineering							4,100.00	4,100.00
	Feb 6	S. Wilson		200.00						200.00
	22	A. Morris		70.00						70.00
3,800.00	23	Morgan & Baldwyn								
	28	Northern Elec.				50.00				50.00
	28	Cash						400.00		400.00
	28	Balance c/d								714.90
6,740.40		Totals	350.10	581.70	20.70	150.00	50.00	800.00	4,100.00	6,767.40
714.90	Mar 1	Balance b/d								

Fig. 102. Part of a typical bank account analysis. There would probably be many of such sheets required. This simple worked example assumes all income was banked and all expenditure was by cheque (which is highly unlikely but convenient for our purposes). If there was income and expediture in cash then a cash analysis would be desirable, but not always possible due to lack of records.

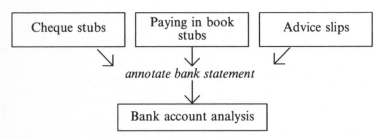

Fig. 103. Annotating the bank statements and then working from them has practical advantages.

69   Bank account analysis step-by-step

What you need:

- Cheque book stubs, paying-in book stubs, bank statements, and any advice slips from the bank explaining entries on the bank statements. The proprietor may have to obtain duplicates of lost bank statements, and his bank will charge for these. He may also have to obtain paid (cancelled) cheques from the bank, where the counterfoils of such cheques have not been filled in.

- Several sheets of wide analysis paper with plenty of columns (e.g. up to 20), including a boldly ruled cash column on each side.

Sort the source documents into date order. Fill in any uncompleted cheque stubs after obtaining the information from cleared cheques or the proprietor's knowledge. Rule off the first bank statement at the date just before the start of the accounting period and do a bank reconciliation as at that date.

Step-by-step

1. Head an analysis sheet: 'Bank Account Analysis for... [business name]... for period... [dates concerned]'.

2. Enter the opening balance from your reconciliation as at the last date of the previous accounting period—not the balance as per the bank statement. (Remember, if the balance is 'in favour' it will go on the left, and vice versa.)

3. Head the first column on the left 'Dr.' and the last column on the right 'Cr.'.

4. List the values of each of the lodgements in the far left hand cash column (Dr.) and the values of each of the cheques in the far right hand column (Cr.). Do this for the whole period covered by the first bank statement. You can take them directly from the bank statements to save time. If most lodgements represent sales revenue you can annotate the exceptions on the bank statement and use it also as a source for analysis later.

5. Add and balance the two columns. Bring forward your balance, just as you would any ledger account.

6. Repeat the process for the period covered by the next bank statement, and so on to the end of the accounting period.

7. Prepare a bank reconciliation statement for the final date of the accounting period.

BANK STATEMENT

Statement as at 31 December 200X

03542256

Date	Particulars		Payments		Receipts		Balance
200X	Opening Balance						350.55
12 Dec	sundry credit				400.00		750.55
15 Dec		543255	25.00				725.55
18 Dec		543256	105.10				620.45
20 Dec	sundry credit				350.50		970.95
28 Dec		543257	10.85				960.10

Fig. 104. Example of an annotated bank statement.

Sales	Particulars	Motor exp	Wages	Rent	Heat/ light	Post tel	Drawgs	Bldg reprs
3,800.00	Sheet 1	350.20	511.50	20.70	150.00	50.00	800.00	4,100.00
2,000.00	2	50.80	500.00	20.70	100.00	50.00	300.00	
1,200.00	3	19.00	800.00	20.70	110.00	10.00	400.00	
7,000.00	Totals	420.00	1,811.50	62.10	360.00	110.00	1,500.00	4,100.00

Fig. 105. Example of a summary of bank account analysis columns.
Note: it does not include the totals columns.

69 Bank account analysis—cont.

8. Extend your bank account analysis to show any extra details (leading to a different balance) shown in your bank reconciliation as at the end of the period (if, of course, the balance is different).

9. Now go back to your first analysis sheet and work your way through analysing each payment and each lodgement into an analysis column, as if it were a day book. The analysis columns for the payments will be credit columns, and those for lodgements will be debit columns: you are analysing the total credit entry to bank account that results from paying all the cheques involved. The double entry principle is not directly involved here; if it were, anlaysis of expenses would not be credit entries. The dividing line between the debit and credit columns will depend on how much of the categories apply to lodgements and payments respectively. Your list of headings, which refer to imaginary ledger accounts, will develop as you go along. You can't decide them all in advance, since you won't know the nature of each transaction until you get to it. You may well run out of analysis columns for payments. Keep one column aside as a 'miscellaneous one'; then you can record any odd bits and pieces there, and analyse them separately on another sheet. To do this, set up a supplementary sheet with the headings you need. Transfer each item by analysing it in the appropriate columns on the supplementary sheet. When all the items have been dealt with enter on the original sheet, in brackets or in red ink, in the miscellaneous column, a figure equal to the column total, to complete the transfer. In the unlikely event that you need a *misc* column on the debit side too, just follow the same procedure.

10. Sum the analysis columns for each sheet.

11. Prepare a summary of analysis column totals for each sheet.

12. Total up the summary columns.

Finishing the job: drawing up final accounts

1. Prepare total debtors and creditors accounts.

2. Extract a trial balance.

3. Adjust for depreciation, bad and doubtful debts, accruals, prepayments, asset disposals and closing stock, obtaining details from the proprietor.

4. Draw up final accounts. Refer to appropriate chapters.

KEY RATIOS AND WHAT THEY MEAN

Concept	Equation	Optimum Value	Diagnostic Value
1. Current Ratio	$\dfrac{\text{Current Assets}}{\text{Current Liabilities}}$	2:1	Test of Solvency: i.e. a Firm's ability to pay its debts
2. Acid Test Ratio	$\dfrac{\text{Current Assets} -\text{Stock}}{\text{Current Liabilities}}$	1:1	A refinement of the above
3. Asset Turnover	$\dfrac{\text{Sales}}{\text{Net Assets}}$	*	Reveals efficiency of asset usage in terms of sales
4. Mark up	Gross Profit as a percentage of cost of goods sold	*	A test of profitability. It reveals whether wholesale prices and other costs of sales are low enough to allow a good level of profit
5. Gross Profit Margin	Gross profit as a percentage of sales	*	As above
6. Net profit Margin	Net profit as a percentage of sales	*	Shows whether overheads are too high to allow a suitable profit
7. RoCE (Return on capital employed)	Net profit margin × asset turnover × 100	*	Of special interest to investors: shows the return on investment in the company
8. Stock turnover	$\dfrac{\text{Cost of goods sold}}{\text{Average Stock}}$	*	Shows how efficiently the firm is using its asset of stock
	If average stock level throughout the year is not known it may be estimated from the average of opening and closing stocks: using closing stock alone is not sastisfactory, since it may be unusually high or low depending on when the last deliveries were made in relation to the Balance Sheet date.		
9. Debt collection period	$\dfrac{\text{Debtors} \times 365}{\text{Sales}}$		Shows how well or badly the firm controls the amount of credit it gives. The lower the better

Note *The higher the better. These optimum values are a rule of thumb only; some firms maintain very different ones without any implication of financial instability or inefficiency. It depends, in the end, on the firm and its aims.

Fig. 106. Key ratios and what they mean.

70 Interpreting accounts

A variety of needs

Different people want to examine a firm's final accounts for different reasons. Final accounts are a means of proving the profits of a business to HM Inland Revenue; but to other users they will mean much more. A purchaser of a business, an investor, a bank or other lender, or a major supplier will study them in detail to discover more information than profit alone. In fact, banks, other lenders and trade creditors will be far more interested in liquidity than profitability. Firms with high profits are not necessarily the most stable ones: often the opposite is true.

The accounts also help the management team. Managers will study interim accounts (accounts produced more than once in the accounting year) as well as the final accounts. They need to compare actual performance and spending figures against budgeted figures, figures of previous periods, figures of competitors and average figures for the size and type of business. They, like other interested parties, will want to check the ratios between different balance sheet items because they can warn of weaknesses in the financial structure of the firm.

Criticism of accounts

An interested party will compare this year's figures with last year's, for example sales and purchases, closing stocks and gross profit as a percentage of sales. How have the key ratios changed from one year to the next? Were changes in the first three of these due to changes in market prices or valuation changes? Or were they due to improved market share or efficiency of operation? Has gross profit as a percentage of sales remained constant in spite of increased turnover?

A high RoCE (return on capital employed) should be investigated: is it realistic? Profits may be inflated by simply over-valuing stocks, through poor estimating of quantities and/or values. There is more than one way of defining RoCE, but the formula shown is a common one. What matters is that the same formula is used consistently when comparing figures, from one period to the next, or one firm to another.

Failure to write down assets properly (vehicles, machinery, etc) or to make enough provision for bad debts (page 105) will also inflate the profits.

A favourable current ratio could also be due to overvaluing stocks or underassessing doubtful debts. The latter would also affect the acid test ratio.

ARMSTRONG ENGINEERING LTD
TRADING, PROFIT & LOSS ACCOUNT
For year ended 31 December 200X

Turnover	308,000
Cost of Sales	177,000
Gross profit	131,000
Administration expenses	54,500
	76,500
Interest payable	900
Profit on ordinary activities before taxation	75,600
Tax on profit from ordinary activities	32,000
Profit on ordinary activities after taxation	43,600
Profit and loss account balance	
Undistributed profits b/f from last year	23,400
	67,000
Proposed dividends	34,500
Undistributed profits c/f to next year	32,500

BALANCE SHEET
as at 31 December 200X

	Cost	Less Provision for Depreciation	Net Book
Fixed assets			
Premises	103,400		103,400
Fixtures and Fittings	10,000	500	9,500
Machinery	40,000	2,000	38,000
Motor Van	10,000	2,000	8,000
	163,400	4,500	158,900
Current assets			
Stock	18,000		
Debtors	48,700		
Cash at Bank	19,850		
Cash in Hand	50		
		86,600	
Less Creditors			
Amounts falling due within 1 yr	22,500		
Accruals	4,000		
Proposed Dividends	34,500	61,000	25,600
Total Net Assets			184,500
Provision for Liabilities and Charges			
Taxation			32,000
Shareholders Funds			
Authorised Share capital			
100,000 Preference Shares of £1	100,000		
100,000 Ordinary Shares of £1	100,000		
	200,000		
Issued Share Capital			
30,000 Preference Shares of £1		30,000	
90,000 Ordinary Shares of £1		90,000	
		120,000	
Capital and Reserves			
Proft & Loss Account balance		32,500	152,500
			184,500

Fig. 107. Final accounts ready for interpretation.

71 Interpreting accounts: example

Take the final accounts of Armstrong Engineering Ltd, shown opposite. Here is an interpretation:

Information	Worked	Example	Comment
Current ratio	$\dfrac{86,600}{61,000}$	= 1.42/1	Rather low
Acid test ratio	$\dfrac{68,600}{61,000}$	= 1.12/1	Acceptable
Asset turnover	$\dfrac{308,000}{184,500}$	= 1.67/1	
Mark-up	$\dfrac{131,000}{177,000}$	× 100 = 74%	Very high
Gross profit margin	$\dfrac{131,000}{308,000}$	× 100 = 43%	Acceptable
Net profit margin	$\dfrac{75,600}{308,000}$	× 100 = 25%	Acceptable
RoCE	0.25 × 1.67 × 100 = 41.75%		
Stock turnover	$\dfrac{177,000}{16,500}$	* = 11 times	Depends on type of business
Debt collection period	$\dfrac{48,700}{308,000}$	× 365 = 58 days	

* This average stock figure is not actually shown in the accounts, because they are *published* ones and it is not required by law to be shown. However, it can be calculated from opening stock and closing stock, both of which will appear in internal accounts. The opening stock figure has been taken from the worked example on page 124.

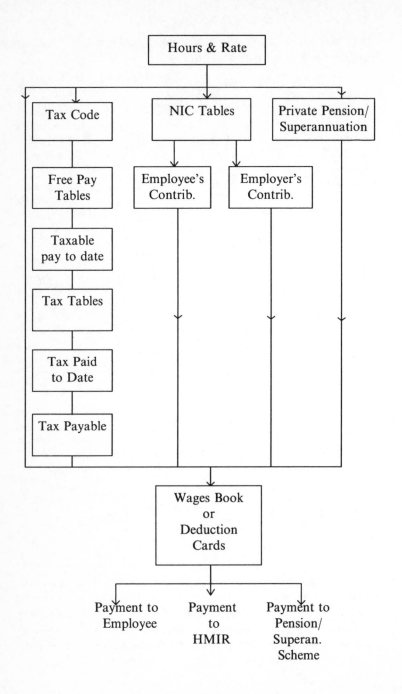

Fig. 108. Wages and salaries at a glance.

72   Wages: basic principles

Wages and salaries are payments for people's labour. They are called **wages** when paid weekly and calculated from the number of hours worked (hourly rates) or units of production finished (piece rates). When payments are made monthly, and there is no direct relationship between them and the hours worked or units produced, they are called **salaries**. Manual and unskilled workers are paid wages; clerical workers, managers and professional people are paid monthly salaries.

Often wage earners are paid a higher hourly rate if they work after the scheduled finishing time; they may be paid an even higher one if they work very unsociable hours. For example, working after 5pm may entitle them to 50% more pay per hour, and they may receive twice the normal rate for work done on a Sunday. These rates are popularly known as 'time and a half' and 'double time'. To find a wage earner's gross pay entitlement the wages clerk multiplies the hours worked by the rate concerned (e.g. 1, 1½ or 2) and then multiplies the product by the hourly pay rate, e.g. £3.50.

Workers usually have to pay income tax on the money they earn. Everyone is entitled to some pay free from tax; the amount of exemption depends on their circumstances. For example people with dependant children have a higher level of tax exemption than those without. This level is called **free pay** and is identified by a **tax code** number. The wages clerk can simply look up the employee's code number and read off against it the cumulative free pay to date (for that tax year) to which that employee is entitled. He then adds this week's pay to total pay to date in the tax year, and deducts from that the free pay to date. He thus arrives at the taxable pay to date. He then calculates, by referring to a table, the cumulative tax payable on this; he deducts from it the tax *actually* paid to date to find out how much tax he must deduct this pay day.

Everyone earning more than a certain level of income (**threshold** level) must also pay regular National Insurance Contributions (NIC), to entitle them to free medical treatment and other state benefits. The wages clerk must also deduct NIC from the wages or salaries paid. The firm itself *also* has to make a contribution to each employee's NIC cover; the amount is related to level of pay.

When an employee earns above a certain figure he is charged a higher tax rate for the amount over that figure. Employee's wages are taxed at source. The company acts as a sort of sub-tax collector for HM Inland Revenue, just as it does for HM Customs & Excise for VAT. Income tax collected at source is called **Pay As You Earn** (PAYE).

WAGES

Suppose Mr Jones works 50 hours, the first 40 of which are at his standard rate of £3.00 p/h, the next 5 of which amount to overtime at 'time and a half' and the next 5 after that represent Sunday work at 'double time'. Suppose also, he pays to a company pension scheme at the rate of 7% of his gross earnings. His wage slip may look something like this.

Hours worked	Standard rate	= 40	=	120.00
	Standard rate × 1½	= 5	=	22.50
	Standard rate × 2	= 5	=	30.00
				172.50
Gross pay				
	Less Income Tax	25.00		
	NIC Contribution	8.63		33.63
				138.87
	Less Pension Scheme Contribution			12.06
	Net Pay			126.81

Fig. 109. Worked example of the completion of a wage slip.

Wages	£20	£10	£5	£1	50p	20p	10p	5p	2p	1p
125.39	120		5			20	10	5	4	
73.40	60	10		3		40				
101.21	100			1		20				1
300.00	280	10	5	4		80	10	5	4	1

Fig. 110. A coin analysis for three wage packets.

73   Coin analysis and wages book

Making up the wage packets

When all the wages have been calculated the wages clerk prepares a **coin analysis**, this is a list of all the coins needed to make up the wage packets (see opposite). Otherwise, how could he make them up? Let's take a simple example. Suppose there are three employees and their wages for a week are £125.39, £73.40, £101.21, a total of £300.00. If the wages clerk merely collected £300 in, say, ten pound notes from the bank he would not be able to make up the wages; he wouldn't have sufficient coins to pay out the amounts; £10s, £5s, 20ps, 10ps, 5ps, and 1ps are all needed in our example.

Wages book/deduction cards

The wages and salaries records of the firm are kept in a **wages book** and/or on **deduction cards** supplied by the Inland Revenue. The records show such details as gross pay to date, free pay to date, taxable pay to date, tax paid to date, and NIC contributions paid to date by employee and employer.

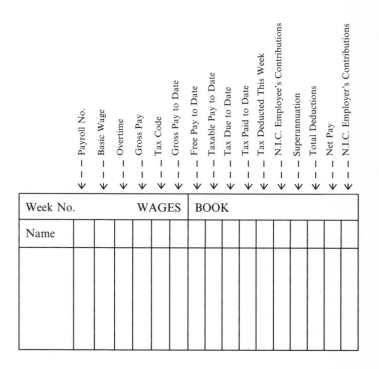

Fig. 111. Example of the layout in a typical wages book.

74 Stock records and valuation

Basic records

Individual stock items can be quite valuable, e.g. household appliances like washing machines or tools like electric drills. In such cases the firm may well want to have a system for booking them in and out of the warehouse whenever they are bought or sold. The supplier's delivery note will be the source document for the booking in; a requisition docket of some kind will be the source document for booking out. So there will always be a record of the stock that should be in hand; periodical physical stock checks (actually going round and counting the stock) will show up any discrepancies arising from errors or pilferage.

Stock valuation methods

At the end of the accounting period stocks have to be valued for the balance sheet. Such value is based on the cost price or replacement price, whichever is the *lower*. The idea is that the asset figures in the accounts should reflect the true values as closely as possible. Each item (or at least each group of items) should be treated separately in this valuation process.

If we are valuing the stock at cost price there may have been a number of price changes throughout the year, and if the goods are identical we may not be able to tell which ones cost which amounts. There are three main ways of dealing with this:

- FIFO (first in first out)
- LIFO (last in first out)
- average cost method.

First in first out

FIFO assumes that the remaining stock is the subject of the most recent prices. Suppose a firm had purchased 30 televisions, the first 10 at £50, another 10 some months later at £55, and near the end of the year another 10 at £60.00. Let's suppose, also, that it sold 15 to one customer, a hotelier perhaps, just before the end of the accounting year. Since 30 had been purchased and only 15 sold there should be 15 left in stock. These 15 would be valued at the prices of the most recently purchased 15; that means all 10 of the most recent purchase at £60 each and 5 of the previous order at £55 each.

	£	£	£
1st Purchase	10 @ 50		500
2nd purchase	10 @ 55		550
			1,050
1st withdrawal	2 @ 50		100
Balance	8 @ 50	400	
	10 @ 55	550	950
2nd withdrawal	8 @ 50	400	
	1 @ 55	55	455
Balance	9 @ 55		495

Fig. 113. Illustration of stock valuation using FIFO.

		£	£
1st Purchase		10 @ 50 =	500
2nd "		10 @ 55 =	550
			1,050

1st withdrawal from warehouse, so average
out the item costs to date, i.e. $\dfrac{1,050}{20}$ = £52.50 each,

Withdrawn 2 @ £52.50

			£
Balance 18 @ £52.50			945
3rd Purchase		10 @ 60 =	600
			1,545

2nd withdrawal from warehouse, so average
out the item costs to date taking the previous
average as the cost of each and every one of the
items purchased before that date, i.e. $\dfrac{1,545}{28}$ = £55.18

Withdrawn 10 @ £55.18

		£
Balance 18 @ £55.18 =		993.24

and so it would go on.

Fig. 114. Stock valuation using 'average cost' method.

Last in first out

LIFO does the opposite. It says that *all* remaining stock on hand is valued at the *earliest* purchase price. To value stock according to LIFO you do the same as for FIFO, using the earliest invoices, instead of the most recent.

Average cost method

The average cost method requires you to divide the remaining stock (numbers of items) into the total cost of all that stock, each time an item is withdrawn from stock. You then apply the cost figure to the withdrawn stock, and to the stock remaining afterwards. When another withdrawal is made you add the last valuation to the cost of all purchases since; you then divide the total by the actual number of items in stock. Again you apply this value to the goods withdrawn *and* to the balance remaining. So the average value of remaining stock may change continuously.

Example

Let's suppose a shop made purchases as in the example; it sells two televisions immediately after the second wholesale purchase and 10 more close to the end of the year. You would then value the stock as shown in the example at the bottom of the opposite page.

FIFO is the most commonly used method. It also seems the most realistic, because businesses usually try to sell their oldest stock first.

75 Encountering deviations from standard methods

This book seeks to teach the principles of double entry book-keeping. However, readers may, in the course of their careers, come across small businesses which use single entry methods.

The Simplex system

The most common single entry method is the **Simplex system**. This is an integrated system involving two books. One is designed for recording daily takings, daily payments and a weekly cash and bank account. All are dealt with on the same page and one page is used per week. The balances of the cash and bank accounts are carried forward to the next week, as the opening figures.

There are special VAT recording arrangements for small businesses. In corner shops for example, it would be burdensome to record each individual item of sale separately—a bar of chocolate to one customer, a newspaper to another and a ballpen to another, for example. In such cases therefore, there are special formulae for computing the VAT payable or repayable. There are a number of different schemes to suit the particular problems of different types of business. In recognition of this the Simplex range contains different versions of the daily takings and purchases book for each scheme.

The second of the two books is a sales and purchases record.

At the end of the daily takings and purchases book there is an analysis section. By following guidance notes printed on the page, owners of businesses can compile their draft profit and loss accounts and balance sheets.

The slip system

As was pointed out on page 13, in double entry book-keeping the sources of information for posting to the ledger are the books of **prime entry**. Nothing should be posted directly from, for example, an invoice, or credit note.

However, this rule is sometimes broken. Occasionally, you'll find this stage bypassed and entries made directly into the ledger. This is called the **slip system**. It is used where accounts have to be kept very up to date, such as in banking and wherever automated systems are used. Where postings are made directly to the ledger, from invoice copies, those copies are filed to form the equivalent of the day book. This I call the **slip + 1 system**, because an extra invoice copy is needed.

In the accounts of some very small firms, the ledgers, too, are sometimes dispensed with. Instead, the invoices (or copies in the case of invoices sent out) are merely filed together with other unpaid ones, in date order. This takes the place of the personal ledger (sales and purchase). When each is paid it is stamped and removed to be filed with all the paid ones. This version I call the **slip + 2 system**, because two additional copies of each invoice are needed.

For the 'slip + 1' version a firm's invoices really need to be printed in triplicate. For the 'slip + 2' version they need to be in quadruplicate.

Fig. 115

A	B	C	D	E	F	G	H	I	J	K	L	M
Date	Particulars	Fo.	Details	Amount		Date	Particulars		Fo.	Details	Amount	
200X						200X						
	=IF(F7<M7,"Balance c/d","")			=IF(F7<M7,M7-F7,"")	=SUM(E3:E6)		=IF(F7>M7,"Balance c/d","")				=IF(M7<F7,F7-M7,"")	=-SUM(L3:L6)
					=SUM(E3:E7)						=SUM(L3:L7)	
	=IF(F7<M7,"Balance b/d","")			=IF(M7<F7,F7-M7,"")			=IF(F7>M7,"Balance b/d","")				=IF(F7<M7,M7-F7,"")	

Fig. 115. This is what your sheet will look like if you command your program to show the formulae you have entered. To do this, click on the Tools menu and select *Options*. Then click on *Formulae* and, finally, click the *OK* button. Don't forget to remove the tick from the *formulas* option after you are satisfied that you have entered the formulae correctly, otherwise your formulae will show instead of your figures.

Fig. 116

Date	Particulars Fo.	Details	Amount	Date	Particulars Fo.	Details	Amount
200X				200X			
Jan-10	Wood		20.00	Jan-31	Cheque		20.00
Jan-15	Nails		2.00				
				31	Balance c/d		2.00
		22.00				22.00	
Feb-01	Balance b/d		2.00				

Fig. 116. This is what your sheet will look like when you have entered figures onto it. You will see that the formulae do not show.

How it works

Nowadays we can use the electronic pages of a spreadsheet program if we have access to a computer. As long as you know how to write on them you can simply follow the instruction in the chapters of this book in the same way as you would for paper pages.

There are various spreadsheet packages on the market, but the differences in the way they work are not great. If you can use one you will be able to grapple with another. The examples used here relate to Microsoft Excel.

Writing on spreadsheet pages

Just as you move to the appropriate spot on a paper page and write on it with a pen, with a spreadsheet page you move to the spot with the direction keys ← ↑ ↓ →

or a mouse and type the information through the keyboard. It's as simple as that.

Adding them up

You will need your standard and formatting toolbars showing. If they are not, click on the view menu and choose the toolbars option. Next, click in the *standard* and *formatting* boxes and then Click 'OK'.

When you come to adding the columns up draw the lines of the answer boxes, using the ⊞ ↓ buttons on the formatting toolbar. Use the arrow key to select a single line for the top and a double line for the bottom. The column will add itself up if you click on the answer box and then click the Σ button on the standard toolbar.

Calculating the c/d balance

Where you have both debit and credit columns you will need to calculate c/d balance. To do this you have to add both sides and take the smaller figure from the larger. Then you enter the difference in the smaller column. That means you've got to jot the two totals down somewhere. Here's how you do that. First make room for a c/d balance by inserting a row if necessary above the answer boxes.

Next insert a column next to the debit column being added, by clicking on the insert menu and choosing the *columns* option while the cursor is to the right of the column. Enter in it the instruction to sum the column immediately above and to its left. To do this click on the Σ button. ' = SUM ( )' will appear in the box. Enter in the brackets the pair of cell references which bound the column you wish to add. Separate them with a colon. Example: E3:E6.

Do the same with the credit column. Example: L3:L6. Here you will find you have to replace a cell reference already showing.

Instructions don't show up on the page – they're invisible – but the answers which they make do. This one is just a jotting though; you don't want it to show, so you must deliberately hide it. You can do this by clicking on the format menu and selecting the *columns* option, then clicking on *hide*, while the cursor is in the column concerned.

Next, enter the '*If*' command. To do this click on the *f** button on the toolbar and choose the '*If*' button while the cursor is in the last space above the total box in the debit column. Click the button labelled *Next*.

Type the first of the two cell references in which you put the column addition formula (i.e. the first of the hidden cells), followed by a < sign, and this is followed by the second of those cell references. Example F7 < M7. In the second box down, marked '*value if true*' type the reverse of this. This time the two cell references should be separated by a minus sign instead of a < symbol. In the third box down simply type a space (press the space bar once). Click the button labelled *Finish*.

Now repeat this on the credit side in the cell above the answer box, reversing the formula.

There is no point in showing zeros in these cells, so if they do appear click on the tools menu and select *options*. Make sure *Zero values* is not ticked and then press the key labelled *OK*.

Next, click in the first of the actual answer boxes and then click on the Σ button twice. Do the same in the right hand answer box.

The balance c/d is then transferred to the opposite side after the total box, as the opening figure (Balance b/d) for the next month. To do this on the spreadsheets just type in the space below the total box on each side the formula which has been entered in the c/d balance box on the opposite side.

Click in the last available space in the particulars column (above the answer box line) and then click the *function* key. Select the *If* option and then, in the dialogue space, type the co-ordinates in which the subtotals are stored in the hidden columns, separated by a ' < ' symbol, (e.g. F7 < M7). In the second dialogue space type 'Balance c/ d'. In the third dialogue box type a space (just press the space below once). Click on finish. Now do the same in the space adjacent to this one on the credit side of the sheet, reversing the formula. Lastly, enter the b/d balance narratives. Using the function key, simply enter in the particulars column, below the totals boxes on each side, the exact formula you entered in the diametrically opposite position (i.e. the space above the total box in the opposite column), but substitute the term c/d with the term b/d.

As you type in the formulae they will appear temporarily in the boxes, but will disappear as soon as you press *finish* in each case.

Configuring a spreadsheet page for day books

It is easy to configure pages which will add themselves up and cross balance for day books. All you have to do is draw in the answer boxes, as you did for the ledger pages. Click on each answer box to highlight it and then click on the Σ button on the toolbar.

Making things easy for yourself

Now you don't have to go through this each month. You can keep this specimen page without any actual monthly figures in it as a template.

Four steps for creating a template

1.   Create a single sheet workbook.
2.   Format it with the titles and formulae.
3.   Save as a template.
4.   Enter the folder in which you wish to store it.

Speeding up ledger posting

You can keep all accounts of a single ledger division (e.g. all customer accounts) on the same sheet, one after the other, as the placing of automated summing and balancing instructions will ensure that the accounts do not get mixed up. Each ledger division becomes a different sheet (e.g. sheet 1 = Sales Daybook, sheet 2 = Nominal Ledger and sheet 3 = Sales Ledger, and so on.) A big advantage of doing this is that you can make posting from daybooks to ledger sheets easy, by putting all the sheets involved on the screen at once. The larger your screen the easier this will be. For example:

• Sales Daybook. • Nominal Ledger. • Sales Ledger.

Then you can simply use copy and paste across the boundaries of the sheets to do your positing. For example, to post a transaction from the Sales Daybook to the relevant ledger sheets, just follow these steps:

1.   Call up all the relevant sheets on the screen at once.
2.   Click on the gross invoice value for each entry on the Sales Daybook sheet.
3.   Press '**Alt**' '**E**' '**C**'.
4.   Scroll down the Sales Ledger sheet to the personal account of the customer concerned.

5. Click on the next available space in the debit column.
6. Press '**Alt**' '**E**' '**P**'.
7. Enter the date in the date column.
8. When all the entries have been posted to the Sales Ledger accounts, proceed as follows.
9. Click on the net total in the Sales Daybook.
10. Press on '**Alt**' '**E**' and '**C**'.
11. Scroll to the next available space in the credit column of the Sales Account in the Nominal Ledger.
12. Press '**Alt**' '**E**' '**P**'.
13. Click on the VAT total in the Sales Daybook and press 'Alt' 'E' 'C'.
14. Scroll to the next available space in the credit column of the VAT account in the Nominal Ledger and press 'Alt' 'E' 'P'.

Automating depreciation calculations
Asset depreciation calculations can be done swiftly and simply, using Excel's built in functions.

Straight line method
Click on the '***f**' tab on the menu bar (this is the toolbar which always shows at the top of the screen).

1. Select the '**Financial**' option.
2. Click, then, on the '**SLN**' option.
3. The following dialogue boxes will appear on the screen:
   asset value; estimated salvage (scrap) value; estimated useful life.
4. Enter the relevant figures and click '**OK**' to find the annual depreciation figure.

Diminishing balance method of depreciation
1. Click on the '**Insert**' tab on the menu bar.
2. Select the '**f***' option.
3. Then select the '**DDB**' option.
4. The following five dialogue boxes will appear.
   cost; estimated salvage value; estimated useful life; start of the period; end of the period.
5. Enter the relevant figures and click on '**OK**' to find the depreciation for the asset.

Sum of the years (or sum of the digits) method of depreciation
Follow the same procedure as for the diminishing balance method, selecting the '**SYD**' instead of the '**DDB**' option.

77 New developments in electronic book-keeping

In previous editions of this book I have showed readers how to make use of the electronic pages of spreadsheets. I have, however, tended to stop short of dealing with computerised book-keeping packages, as they were, hitherto, rather too complicated for many people. Things have changed though; there are now various packages on the market to suit all needs and various ability and skill levels. A comprehensive book-keeping course book must now give some attention to these too.

Their use is not a substitute for a thorough knowledge of book-keeping, however. It is not much use having accounts if you don't know what they mean and how to use them to control your business. Their use will merely speeds things up and take the donkeywork out of the job.

The industry standard product has, for long, been Sage Accounting Systems and there are a number of versions to suit different needs. Sage Accounting Systems used to be quite complicated, but things have changed here. The entry-level Sage Accounting System is now a product called *Instant Accounts 8*. This works on *Windows 98* and above. It completes all of the standard books, it does your credit control automatically, completes your VAT records, converts from pounds to euros and vice versa and keeps supplier and customer records.

Sage Instant Accounts 8 plus has all that *Instant Accounts 8* has plus a bit more. It integrates with *Microsoft Office* and it is email and Web enabled.

Then there is Sage's *TAS bookkeeper*. This is much cheaper and it is another option for a first place to start in computerising your accounts. It is a simple and basic system, but it is easy to learn and use.

For larger businesses and people with more computer skills, there is *Sage Instant Business Suite* package. It does all that *Instant Accounts 8* does, plus payroll records, employee records and statutory forms.

A package that some of the banks promote is *Quicken*. This is considerably cheaper than other packages at only £16.95, but while it is useful for business accounts, it is really more appropriate for personal finances. It can handle bank account management, including bank reconciliation and savings and asset management. The wizard it has is very helpful.

One of the best systems around is *Simply Books*. This is less complicated than many other systems. It is quick to install; it takes only about two minutes. it works on *Windows 95* and above. This is a virtually idiot-proof system. The instructions are very simple and the spreadsheet type pages, such as are seen in Chapter 76 of this book, make new users feel at home if they are familiar with using *Microsoft Excel*.

It is designed for sole traders and small businesses, with up to five employees, so it is obviously stripped down to the basics. However, it does all the standard books of account, prints invoices, records them automatically and it shows your bank reconciliation.

Glossary

Accounting ratios. Statistical measures taken from the accounts of a business to aid financial assessment and control.

Accruals. Expenses incurred, but not yet billed to the firm.

Amalgamation. Joining two firms into one.

Assets. The term comes from the word 'assez', meaning 'enough'. It is used because the property of a proprietor is judged in terms of whether it is sufficient to discharge his liabilities, i.e.: to settle his debts.

Assets: fixed and current. Assets are classified into fixed assets and current assets. The former are those which will be retained in the business, e.g.: machines, motor vehicles, etc; the latter, it is assumed, will be consumed in the business within the fiscal year and includes: stock, debtors, cash in hand and cash at bank.

Average cost method. A method of stock valuation in which remaining stock values are averaged out every time a withdrawal is made.

Bad debts. Debts which a firm regards as uncollectable.

Balance. This term is used in 3 different ways in double entry book-keeping.
1. For the debit and credit column totals
2. For the balancing item required to equalise the two column totals (balance c/d)
3. For that balancing item transferred as the opening figure for   the subsequent accounting period (balance b/d).

Balance sheet. A listing of the ledger balances remaining after compilation of the revenue account. (It is not, as some think, called a balance sheet merely because it balances.)

Bank reconciliation. A standardised format statement explaining a discrepancy between the bank statement balance and the cash book balance.

Bought ledger. That division of the ledger which contains personal accounts of suppliers. It is also sometimes referred to as the purchase ledger or creditors account.

Cash book. The book in which records of cash and banking transactions are made.

Credit note. A document which reverses the effect of an invoice.

Creditors. People or firms to whom the business owes money.

Capital. This term derives from the latin words 'Capitalis', meaning 'chief' and 'capitali', meaning 'property', giving us the combined meaning of 'property of the chief'. The chief of a business is, of course, the proprietor.

Control account. An account in a ledger division which amounts to a mini trial balance for that division. It consists of aggregates of each type of posting therein, e.g.: the sales ledger control account will be posted with the aggregate value of cheques received, the aggregated invoice totals for the month, and so on. It is used both as a check on the accuracy and as a means of making the compilation of the overall trial balance easier.

Debtors. People or firms who owe money to the business.

Depreciation. The writing down of an asset's value in the books of a business to allow for wear and tear.

Dividends. Shares of profit paid to shareholders.

Drawings. The retrieval of capital by a proprietor or partners for private use.

Early settlement discount. A discount allowed to customers as an enticement to pay their bills on time.

Expenses. Purchases of goods or services for consumption by the business within the financial year. They do not enhance the value of any fixed assets though they may include repairs to them. Examples are: goods for resale, wages, repairs, heat and lighting costs, petrol and professional fees.

FIFO. 'First In First Out'. A method of stock valuation based on the assumption that the latest cost prices prevail.

Final accounts. The revenue accounts and balance sheet of a firm at a particular moment in time and covering a particular financial period, e.g.: a financial year.

Goodwill. The intangible fixed asset of a business's reputation.

Gross profit. Sales revenue minus cost of sales.

Gross profit margin. Gross profit as a percentage of sales.

Imprest system. A system of managing petty cash in which a fund is regularly replenished to a set amount by the cashier.

Income and expenditure account. A non-profit-making club's equiv-alent of a business's profit and loss account.

Input tax. VAT charged by a supplier on goods or services it has supplied and which will be subsequently reclaimed by the business from HM Customs and Excise.

Interim accounts. Revenue accounts and balance sheet drawn up at intervals more frequent than each financial year and used for management purposes.

Invoice. A bill for goods or services rendered.

Journal. A book of prime entry in debit and credit format used for initial entries of a miscellany of transactions for which no other book exists. E.g.: the intial recording of opening figures, bad debt, depreciation and the correction of errors. However, some people refer to the day books as journals too, e.g.: sales journal, purchase journal, etc. and the journal as defined above is then referred to as the 'Journal Proper'.

Ledger. The ledger is the essential double entry accounting system and consists of a number of divisions, e.g.: the general ledger, personal ledger, cash book and petty cash book. Since each of these divisions is often kept in a separate bound book it is not surprising that people tend to think of them as separate ledgers, but this is not truly the case, they are all divisions of the one ledger system.

Liabilities. Financial obligations to others—debts owed out. Capital too is listed under liabilities in the balance sheet since it is owed to the proprietor by the business.

LIFO. Last In First Out. A method of stock valuation based on the assumption that the earliest cost prices prevail.

Limited Company. A business entity which has its own rights and obligations under the law. Its capital is divided into shares and the liability of the shareholders in the event of a liquidation is limited to the value of shares held.

Liquidity. The ability of a firm to pay its debts.

Net profit. Gross profit minus overhead expenses.

Nominal ledger. That division of the ledger in which impersonal accounts are kept.

Output tax. VAT charged to customers by a business and which it will have to subsequently remit to HM Customs and Excise.

Overhead expenses. Expenses which cannot be directly related to turnover.

Partnership. An unlimited business unit owned by more than one proprietor.

Personal ledger. That division of the ledger which contains personal accounts of suppliers and customers. It is divided into 2 subdivisions—bought ledger and sales ledger.

Petty cash book. The book of prime entry in which records of small cash transactions are kept.

Postage book. A book in which records of stamps purchased and used are made.

Private ledger. A separate division of the ledger in which capital items are posted.

Private limited company. A limited liability company whose share dealings are restricted and cannot be quoted on the stock exchange. It only has to have two shareholders and one director to comply with company law, though that director could not also act as company secretary.

Profit. The reward to the proprietor, partners or shareholders for the business risk they have taken.

Profit and loss account. That section of the revenue accounts which shows the calculation of net profit, by deduction of overhead expenses from gross profit.

Profit and loss appropriation account. That part of the revenue accounts of a partnership or limited company which explains how the net profit is to be appropriated.

Provision for bad debts. A suitable provision set against the value of debtors to allow for some which will become uncollectable.

Provision for depreciation. An allowance set against an asset for wear and tear.

Public company. A limited liability company which is empowered to sell its shares freely and have them quoted on the stock exchange. It must have a minimum of 7 shareholders and 2 directors.

Purchase day book. A book of prime entry in which the inital record of purchases is made prior to posting to the ledger.

Purchase returns day book. A book of prime entry in which the intial record of goods returned to suppliers is made prior to posting to the ledger.

Receipts and payments book. The main accounting book used by many club stewards in non-profit-making clubs.

Revenues. Inflows of money or money's worth to the firm, e.g. sales figures, rents, discounts received etc. They must be distinguished from proceeds of sale of fixed assets, which is capital income rather than revenue income and is ultimately shown in the balance sheet rather than the trading, profit and loss account.

Revenue accounts. The set of accounts which shows the net profit earned by a business, how it is calculated and how it is to be distributed. Typically they include the trading account and the profit and loss account. For a partnership or limited company they will also include an appropriation account, for a manufacturing business, they will include the manufacturing account and for a club they will include an income and expenditure account.

Sales day book. The book of prime entry in which the initial record of all sales is made prior to posting to the ledger.

Sales ledger. That division of the ledger which contains personal accounts of customers. It is also sometimes referred to as the debtors ledger.

Sales return day book. The book of prime entry in which the initial record of goods returned by customers is made prior to posting to the ledger.

Share capital.

Authorised share capital The amount of capital a company is permitted to raise by means of issuing shares.

Issued share capital The nominal value of shares actually issued by a company.

Ordinary shares Shares in a company which earn the holders a percentage of profits. In the event of a liquidation this category of investors will be the last in the queue for recovery of their investment.

Preference shares Shares which entitle the holders to a fixed rate of dividend on profits. Their claim on profits comes before ordinary shareholders as would their claim on residual assets in the event of a liquidation.

Redeemable shares Shares which the company is empowered to buy back.

Sole proprietorship. An unlimited firm owned solely by one person.

Statement of affairs. A description and valuation of the assets and liabilities of a business and the way the net assets are represented by capital at a particular moment in time. In effect, it is the same as a balance sheet, but not called so because the source used for compilation is not the ledger balances, but rather a series of inventories.

Stock. Goods for resale or for use in a manufacturing process for the production of goods for resale.

Suspense account. An account into which a value equal to an error can be posted temporarily in order to make the books balance while the source of the error is being sought.

Trading account. That section of the revenue accounts which explains the calculation of gross profit.

Trial balance. A listing and summing of all the ledger balances at a particular moment in time to confirm that the total debits equal the total credits and, thus, provide some measure of confidence in the accuracy of the ledger posting.

Value Added Tax (VAT). A tax on goods and services. Businesses act as sub-collectors by charging VAT on goods they sell and remitting it to HM Customs and Excise after deducting the VAT they, themselves, have been charged on their purchases from other firms.

Working capital. The difference between current assets and current liabilities.

Index